FISH QUAY FOLK
of NORTH SHIELDS

Daniel M Turner

With Best Wishes

Daniel Turner.

White Wings
PUBLISHING

First published 2014 by White Wings Publishing, North Shields,
Tyne and Wear, England

www.whitewingspublishing.co.uk

Copyright © Daniel M Turner 2014

Photographs Copyright © Daniel M Turner (unless stated otherwise)

ISBN 978-0-9930205-0-6

A catalogue record for this book is available from the British Library.

The right of Daniel M Tuner to be identified as the author and proprietor of this
work has been asserted by him in accordance with the Copyright, Designs and
Patents Act 1988.

The front cover shows *Luc* (SN 36) returning to port. Photograph © Daniel M Turner
(see page 41 for full caption).

The back cover photograph of the author was taken by Raj Bhatia (2013)

Designed and typeset by Raspberry Creative Type, Edinburgh

Printed by Elanders Ltd,
Merlin Way, New York Business Park, North Tyneside NE27 0QG

Herring gull

Mackerel

HERRING GIRLS AND FISH BARRELS
Fish quay metalwork, designed by artist Maureen Black, shows fisher girls (from years gone by)
storing herrings in barrels with salt. Photographed on 19 May 1991

Contents

Foreword by Jeremy Pritchard		i
1	Clifford Joseph Ellis B.E.M.	9
2	Douglas Brunton Clark	27
3	Eileen McConnell	43
4	Jackie Weatherstone	55
5	Kevin Mole	69
6	Michael Nugent	77
7	Michael Smith	87
8	Rob Dearman	99
9	Roy Elliott	115
10	Stuart Brown	125
11	Tommy Bailey	135
12	Tony Asiamah	143
13	Trevor Fryer	159
References		175
Miscellaneous internet sites utilised		176
Acknowledgements		177

FISH QUAY VIEW
Looking across the river with (from left): the Gut with larger fishing vessels at rest, fish quay extension, white New Low Light rising and Knott's Flats on the bank top behind, 8 June 2013

HORSE MACKEREL
A Scad (or Horse Mackerel) on the morning fish quay market, 3 December 2012

Foreword

In the twenty years I worked at North Shields Fish Quay I doubt a week passed without my running into Dan Turner at some point, invariably dressed for the vagaries of the North Sea weather, binoculars around his neck, a backpack and, of course, his trademark camera tripod balanced across his shoulder. We would swap notes; me to tell him how the trawlers and the trade were faring; he to give me the latest on what migratory birds were passing through the area at the time. As a familiar and friendly face he engaged widely and over time became more involved in the local scene, particularly on behalf of the RNLI.

So, how did he get from there to write this book? Well, the Fish Quay is rather like a family, perhaps a little dysfunctional at times, but a family for all that; and like so many community families up and down the land it adopts a new member every now and again. We don't know when it was exactly that Dan was so adopted ... the Fish Quay does graduals, not exacts, but he was, and as a member he is now one for life. And it's that membership, with its unlocked and open doors, that has given Dan the opportunity to write this collection of biographies illustrating the diverse nature of Fish Quay life. Dan's subjects are a cross-section of local characters: fishermen, local traders, lifeboatmen, naturalists; they tell the story of a generation that pre-dates the digital age, of people who take nothing for granted and understand that everything has to be earned. These are interesting lives, full of endeavour, graft and purpose and I hope you will enjoy reading them as much as I have and that maybe Dan can be encouraged to produce a second volume.

Jeremy Pritchard

ADVENTURE AT SUNSET
Geoff Nugent's fishing vessel *Adventure* (BH 2) in the Gut at North Shields fish quay
as the sun sets, 22 October 2006. In the top right corner of the photograph the tall
disused ice plant rises from the west quay, just left of the old Stag Line building on the
bank top

MARKET HADDOCK
Fresh haddock on the morning fish quay market, 20 August 2012

Clifford Joseph Ellis, B.E.M.

Retired Grimsby and North Shields fisherman – awarded the British Empire Medal in 1988

Cliff was born (on 2 March 1936) in Grimsby and left school at the age of fourteen and a half when his mother found him a job washing wooden fish boxes at Grimsby docks. He worked five days a week, and remembered that "no fish was landed at the weekend." His working hours were from six in the morning to between seven and ten in the evening. While working there he trained for a certificate in preliminary cooking and he told the author that he "left within a week of getting this certificate." He then joined the vessel *Northern Rover* as a 'deckie learner'. Cliff recalled this fishing boat was first named *Indian Star* and later renamed to *White Sea*; he also referred to her as *Northern Star*. He had been going to join *Northern Rover* as a galley boy (cook), but their deckie learner went missing – so he "grabbed" that position as it earned more money. He said that as galley boy it would have been interesting as "you only needed to prepare three meals: breakfast, dinner and tea. Then you would be able to spend time in the wheelhouse and the fish room."

Cliff became a fisherman at the age of fifteen and continued until eighteen at Grimsby. He was then called up for two years National Service with the army. Enjoying the life so much he signed up for a third year. He first served in Berlin and later in Malaya

PORTRAIT
Beside Lloyd's jetty, with the Tyne river mouth behind, including Tynemouth pier and the Black Middens, 20 May 2012

9

– where he saw active service. Starting out as a Private he was promoted to Lance Corporal, but later left after a spell at Chilwell HQ in Nottingham. He had just returned from an infantry battalion (on active service) with very strict discipline and the change to a more relaxed environment was "too much" for him, so he left.

Before joining, and after leaving, the army Cliff's work aboard Grimsby trawlers included experience with the following vessels:

- *Northern Rover*   during June 1952 - April 1953
- *Grimsby Town*   during April 1953 - June 1954
- National Service came during the period: 1954 - 1957
- *Stafnes*   during August - October 1958, as deckhand
- *Rinovia*   during November 1958 - 1959, as deckhand

Later, on 30 March 1961, Cliff was registered as 'Mate', and his Grimsby service continued with experiences aboard:

- *Roda*   during April - May 1961
- *Streymoy*   during May 1961 - January 1962, as deckhand (Julian Egholm, from the Faeroes, was skipper)
- *Mercator*   during January - May 1962, as deckhand

Cliff recalled that when the UK was "chucked out of Iceland," (following the First Cod War) the Grimsby fishermen had to look for alternative employment. So he came to North Shields for a better chance of fishing after the Grimsby boats became laid up as they were unable to fish in Icelandic waters. The North Shields boats were fishing in the North Sea. He said he "arrived at North Shields from Grimsby aboard the Danish fishing vessel called *Roda*". When he landed here he had a look around and spoke with Norman Morse, of the fishing vessel *Contesta*. Norman (also known as Norrie) said he was looking for a good bloke, so Cliff replied "Well you have seen him now!" When Cliff returned to port a few weeks later he found a letter from Norrie saying that if he was still interested in the job it was his. *Contesta* was upriver at Coble Dene dock getting fitted out for a couple of weeks when Cliff joined the vessel. Cliff said, "It was strange going to sea with Geordies. They had a different outlook to what I was used to." Cliff reported of working with *Contesta* when he got his skipper's ticket.

Cliff's North Shields fishing experiences in the ensuing years soon progressed with three vessels as discussed here. He was awarded his skipper's ticket (also denoted as a 'Certificate of Competency – Second Hand Special') on 18 March 1966. This allowed him to act as skipper on vessels up to 50 tons and was issued by the Ministy of Transport / Board of Trade. Time followed as skipper and mate aboard three local trawlers: *Concord*, *Contesta* and *Conmoran* which were all owned by the Morse brothers – Alan and Norman. The Morse brothers also owned *Conduan* and *Congener* as well as being North Shields skippers and acting as Cliff's employers for some time. Cliff also had a spell with Jackie Dowse (skipper) on Jackie's vessel *Condowan*.

SECOND HAND (SPECIAL)
Cliff's certification as a skipper of fishing boats, granted on 18 March 1966

Cliff was skipper with *Concord* for six months, and on this vessel he first learnt how to work in the role of skipper. He described her as "a good sea boat, but not suitable for fishing in January and February" i.e. in peak winter weather conditions. So he progressed to the larger vessel *Contesta* which he skippered for one or two years before moving on to *Conmoran*. With *Conmoran* Cliff was 'mate' from the late 1960s to 1974. Following his time with the boats of Alan and Norman Morse, Cliff moved on to skipper North Shields vessel *Lindisfarne* for two years from 1974 to 1976. He became part-owner of this fishing vessel along with Richard Irvin. He then advanced to skipper the *Christene Nielsen* (GY 298), from 1976 to 1998, and became a part-owner along with Volma Nielsen and Richard Irvin.

Cliff took a photograph on the *Conmoran*, when he was mate and Alan Morse (senior) was skipper. The photograph shows some of the crew with fish on the side of the boat – there was a total crew of seven men. As mate, Cliff looked after the fish and was in charge of gutting (spending a lot of time on this task!), storage and landing boxes at port. These trips during the 1960s from North Shields on *Conmoran* were of four to five days in length. On most of these trips Cliff said he "went straight down to the fish room" below the deck. The photograph is reproduced here.

AWASH WITH FISH
The *Conmoran* as her crew sort the catch on deck. Cliff was 'mate' with the *Conmoran* from the late 1960s to 1974.
Photograph by Cliff Ellis

The *Christine Nielsen*, steel-built in 1975 at Esbjerg (Denmark), was launched in 1976. Cliff still has the wine list, printed on parchment, from the reception meal and celebration for the boat's launch at Esbjerg. The vessel was part-owned by the Nielsen family, from Esbjerg. Mr Volma Nielsen was part-owner and lived just north of the town. The launch reception was held near Esbjerg harbour. Christine Nielsen was the name of Volma's daughter. Volma Nielsen fished off Iceland during the Second World War and became owner of several fishing vessels which he named after gold mining regions in Alaska – for example *Kiana*, *Susitna* and *MV Matanuska*. Cliff mentioned that Volma owned fourteen vessels at one time, and when he fished in Icelandic waters he would land the catch at Fleetwood. "He was a great seaman," confirmed Cliff.

The following notes record some of the times while Cliff skippered the *Christine Nielsen*, fishing out of North Shields. Her normal fishing trips were of ten days duration.

Cliff took a summer-time photograph, around 1976, after he first took charge of the *Christine Nielsen* and when she was surrounded by fulmars about 200 miles ESE of the Tyne. He used to take the vessel to fish at the areas named Silver Pits and Cleaver

LINDISFARNE (BCK 147)
Berthed at the fish quay on 11 October 1987. Cliff was skipper of this vessel from 1974 - 1976

CHRISTINE NIELSEN AT ESBJERG
Looking smart at Esbjerg harbour, Denmark, soon after her launch, 1976. Photograph courtesy of Cliff Ellis

Bank. Cliff recalled that fulmars at this time were a regular feature throughout the year, with more present in the winter, and they would spread to about a mile radius around his ship. Some of the fulmars received injuries when the ropes left the boat, during the shooting of the nets. Occasionally birds would suffer a broken wing in this way, but there was nothing the crew could do to stop it. Cliff told the author that there came a time when they started to gut the fish aboard and store the innards to pour out on the sea later so the fulmars would not get injured as often. Then, when the large quantities of offal were discarded overboard, very many fulmars would descend upon them to feed voraciously. Fulmars loved the massive livers from the large cod. The livers would float on the sea and the fulmars were savage with each other fighting over them, often standing on top of each other to get to them. Danish vessels had barrels on board where cod livers were stored to take ashore for the making of cod liver oil. Cliff remembered that normally fulmars would be the first bird to attend *Christene Nielsen* in the early morning.

FULMARS COME TO FEED
All around *Christine Nielsen* fulmars rest – waiting to feed as the catch is hauled, gutted and stored. Photograph by Cliff Ellis, summer ca. 1976

Soon after Cliff started with the *Christine Nielsen*, one winter (which may have actually been in the early 1980s) the southeast North Sea was frozen for about four weeks.

COLD WINTER WEATHER
Esbjerg-registered fishing vessel (E 709), in Esbjerg harbour, covered in ice. Cliff sailed the *Christine Nielsen* here in convoy with Danish trawlers through sea ice in the late 1970s or early 1980s. Photograph courtesy of Cliff Ellis

Cliff tried to steam for Esbjerg and was unable to get through the sea ice as it was frozen to a distance of fifty miles offshore (off Blåvand). Ice formed on the structure of his ship and the hydraulic oil froze too, so he headed for Esbjerg to get his vessel fixed. He joined a convoy of larger Danish industrial trawlers that were able to break a way through the ice, which the *Christine Nielsen* was too small to do alone. There were ten to fifteen vessels in the convoy and Cliff followed at the rear sailing his boat to port. During this incident the sea ice grew to six inches in thickness. The men on the fishing boats used pick axe shafts to break the ice accumulating on their vessels. The author wonders whether these entries, from Cliff's 1982 log book, may reference this incident:

"Thursday 7 January" Two hauls were made, totalling 67 boxes of fish, and then the log records "Seal broke port aft drum. Went into Esbjerg for repair. Land fish. Weather bad frost 28 degrees below. Left 1500 hrs. Steamed west to defrost ship out." Then came the entry for "Saturday 9 January. Steaming back to Helgoland. Ship defrosted."

Other possible winters when this icing incident may have occurred were 1976-1977, 1977-1978 and 1978-1979. In each of these winters there are gaps in his small log book entries which may account for the occurrence.

Another of Cliff's own photographs shows an old fishing net hauled up in the net which was being used to catch fish from his boat. The old net had been a 'set' (or 'gill') net which would have been set at the bottom of the sea by the Danish fishermen. This net must have been lost and abandoned for some time in the sea. When it was brought to the surface it held many dead fish, showing how it continued to catch fish and act as a danger. At Vitsanna (or White Sands – off the Danish coastline), one of Cliff's crew photographed a stranded fishing vessel on the sands. One of her crew had fallen asleep and when they awoke in the morning their boat was on the shore. The picture is reproduced here.

Once, the Christine Nielsen was involved in a collision when 'dodging' to a buoy in thick freezing fog one winter night, off the Heligoland Bight. Dodging is when the engine is ticking over at a slow speed. This was Saturday 19 January 1980, and Cliff's log records "Rammed by German ship M S Stokkon Fels. 19:20 hrs. WSW Helgoland." Repairs must have been made at port and the next entry shows Christine Nielsen sailing four weeks later with a crew of eight on Saturday 16 February.

When the Alexander L. Kielland, a semi-submersible drilling rig, capsized at sea in late March 1980, the Christine Nielsen went to join the rescue. The floating drilling rig was being used to provide living quarters for offshore workers. Cliff steamed north for forty miles, from where he had been fishing, to the EkoFisk oil grounds. The normal radio range for vessels at sea was about thirty miles, but Nimrod aircraft from the RAF were involved in the rescue and their additional height meant that radio signals could be received for a greater distance. The crew of the Christine Nielsen retrieved a body from the water. The unfortunate man must have been alive for a long time in the water as he had wrapped a rope around his waist several times and tied this to a type of buoy floating in the sea. The sea must have been uncompromising

HELIGOLAND
The *Christine Nielsen* called occasionally at this German archipelago when fishing in the North Sea. Photograph courtesy of Cliff Ellis

STRANDED
Danish fishing boat (RI 243: Port of Registry – Ringkøbing) stranded at Vitsanna, Denmark, date unknown. One of the crew had fallen asleep at night. Photograph courtesy of Cliff Ellis

– the man's waist was much bruised and injured by the rope he had tied around himself. Cliff remembered a strong easterly motion of the sea during this rescue, moving bodies eastwards … 123 people died. Skipper Cliff recalled a large northerly swell and a massive storage tank in the sea at the oil field which received oil from nine rigs – all linked to it from many directions. The additional swell, caused by this huge tank falling and rising in the body of the water, was dangerous. As the *Christine Nielsen* crew handed over the body to a small launch, from a naval ship or rig support vessel, the additional swell from the edge of the tank in the water, rising and falling, made conditions difficult for the handover. Another fishing vessel that came to assist in the rescue sadly collected three bodies from the sea before steaming for

port. Cliff's log entry for Friday 27 March 1980 stated "Looking for survivors from Edda oil field. Picked up one man dead. Also liferaft." His log entry for the next day shows their vessel was fishing again, making 28 boxes from six hauls. For the first haul on Saturday 28 March, the log states "Came fast and parted. No fish."

ALEXANDER L. KIELLAND ACCIDENT
Cliff steamed north to help in the search for survivors when the semi-submersible rig capsized. The picture shows a launch which came to the *Christine Nielsen* to collect a body the crew had recovered from the sea, 27 March 1980. Photograph by Cliff Ellis

CHRISTINE NIELSEN (GY 298)
At sea, date unknown. Cliff was skipper and part-owner from 1976 - 1998. Photograph courtesy of Cliff Ellis

Cliff recounted that when fishing with the *Christine Nielsen*, across the front of the net on the sea bed was a line 240 feet in length. Usually such net tows were two to three hours in length. The net would be a mile away from the trawler when towing and they would haul it in by pulling, or winching, on two ropes together (one at each side of the net). Cliff would check the ropes attached to the net from the wheelhouse to ensure the same length was above the water on each side of the net … making it level. The deeper the net was in the water meant a steeper incline of the ropes leaving the ship, and as the net was winched-in the rope would become steeper since the net clung to the sea bottom. Seine net ropes are now made from a combination of synthetic fibres as these do not rot like natural fibres. Hemp ropes were used when Cliff first started fishing on the *Christine Nielsen*, but they were of poor quality and expensive. Sisal rope was also used in the early days, due to the expense of hemp. Sisal (*Agave sisalana*) is a species of agave whose fibre is traditionally used for rope and twine. Then they progressed on to use the synthetic seine net rope. In addition a combination rope was used at one time which was composed of both rope and

APPROACHING THE FISH QUAY
Christine Nielsen (GY 298) approaches North Shields fish quay, 16 July 1986

wire. Sometimes, Cliff told the author, he fished with a low full moon – this seemed to produce good conditions for dab and plaice.

At one time the echo sounder on *Christine Nielsen* was a Simrad EQ – which showed an echo where many cod were present and Cliff would record the position of these soundings / marks for future reference. Plotter roll charts were used for recording 'shoots' of the nets and the position in the sea through the Decca lanes. Cables from Cliff's ship were connected to the net and transducers connected to the headline in order to record positions. Such readings would show exactly where the net was in the water with no need for the skipper to guess. The otter boards Cliff used at one time, for holding open the net mouth, were called Suberkrub doors (after inventor Franz Suberkrüb). Cliff recalled that the government fisheries people would provide, if asked, specific measurements for net making, associated winch powers to use, and much more information to help with different types of fishing. He recounted that at one of the fishing grounds where they fished, some dredgers came to take away rocks, boulders and gravel. This ruined a large area of fishing grounds – after the suction of this material from the sea bed.

Cliff was the first fisherman to determine that North Sea fish were shoaling around oil and gas pipes. He described to the author how the pipes are about eighteen inches in diameter and are not buried in the sea bed, but just above the surface. He could identify where the pipes were, through echo soundings, and used to follow them and mark their positions. His catches of fish along the lengths of the pipes with the *Christine Nielsen* were extremely good, and he would return time after time to fish at these locations. He kept this knowledge a closely guarded secret, eventually telling another fisherman from Scarborough. This fisherman then started fishing the pipes and eventually this fish behaviour became common knowledge and all the fishermen started to follow the pipes. Along the pipelines Cliff would particularly catch cod, but also made large hauls of dogfish and had good catches of coley (saithe).

Cliff and his crew were very successful at catching fish! His logs for 1983 and 1984 record gross landings for each of these years of over £400,000. One of Cliff's regular small annual log books was purchased from Harry Smith & Company, Commercial Stationers & Printers, Nile Street, North Shields. His notes for the year of 1985 show landings grossing over £70,000 in the months of March and October. Logs from this period also show a refit aboard his boat in summer 1983 and 1985. There were

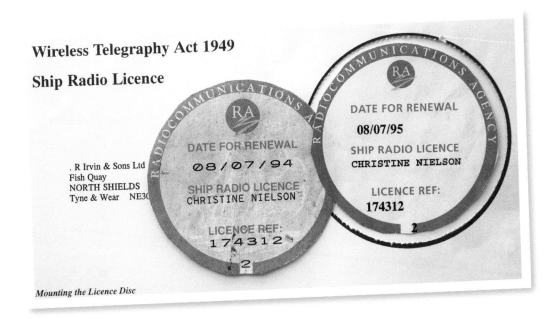

Wireless Telegraphy Act 1949

Ship Radio Licence

. R Irvin & Sons Ltd
Fish Quay
NORTH SHIELDS
Tyne & Wear   NE3C

DATE FOR RENEWAL
08/07/94
SHIP RADIO LICENCE
CHRISTINE NIELSON
LICENCE REF:
174312
2

DATE FOR RENEWAL
08/07/95
SHIP RADIO LICENCE
CHRISTINE NIELSON
LICENCE REF:
174312
2

Mounting the Licence Disc

RADIO LICENCES
Ship radio licences for the *Christine Nielsen* from July 1994 and July 1995

often repairs to make. Cliff's 1979 log entry for Wednesday 28 February records "2 haul today. Poor weather. Repaired rope drums all day." Log entry for Wednesday 28 July 1982 recorded "Sailed. Left 1600 hours. Tried one haul. Pipeline. 36 mile. No Good too many jellies" i.e. jellyfish. Examples of two days of catches are shown by the following extracts from the 'Vessel Catch Log Book':

On 14 July 1984 there were eight hauls, each of roughly two hours duration, between 03:45 and 20:45. The fishing method on that occasion was with seine net. Live fish weight (in kilograms) caught that day was recorded as: 4420 of cod, 930 of haddock, 290 of plaice, 550 of lemon sole and 65 of others. Position of first haul was at 56° 37.15 N and 03° 07.77 E and last haul was at 56° 26.23 N and 02° 25.25 E, all fishing this day was in zone IVB

When trawling on 1 June 1994 there were three net shoots and hauls between 03:00 and 21:00. The three hauls were noted with estimated fishing times of 5 ¾ hours, 5 and 6 hours. These hauls brought aboard live weights of: 1512 kilograms of cod, 108 of cat fish and 162 of others (i.e. 54 of lemon sole and 108 of ling). Position for first net shoot was at 56° 24.50 N and 02° 51.50 E which was later hauled at 56° 39.00 N and 02° 41.50 E, all fishing this day was in zone IVB

A third example (dated 1 August 1993) is shown in the photograph on next page.

TRIP NO. THREE   DATE OF HAULS 1-8-93   DETAILS OF GEAR SEINE NET   PAGE № 9609

Time of Haul	Position of Haul	Estimated Fishing Time	Zone	Cod	Haddock	Whiting	Plaice	Coley	LEMON	Others	Est. of Discards
BST 0345	56° 40.50 / 02° 41.00	2	IVB	174	108						NIL
0600	56° 40.25 / 02° 39.00	2	IVB	58	108		50				NIL
0820	56° 38.00 / 02° 41.00	2	IVB	174	54		50	50			NIL
1045	56° 36.00 / 02° 42.50	2	IVB	116	378				50		NIL
1300	56° 36.00 / 02° 45.00	2	IVB	232	216		50				NIL
1500	56° 34.80 / 02° 46.00	2	IVB	174	162				50		NIL
1810	56° 31.50 / 02° 45.50	2	IVB	232	54		50				NIL
			Daily Total	1160	1080		200	50	100		
			Zone..........								
			Zone..........								
			All Areas								
			Trip/Running Total	9214	5726		1200	150	750	100	
			Zone..........								
			Zone..........								
			All Areas								
			Transhipments								

Remarks & Record of Radio Reports

Inspected 010893 by T. GRIMSTAD 14M OK.

K/V NORDSJØBAS
KYSTVAKTSKVADRON SØR
BOKS 1
5078 HAAKONSVERN   Position 56 30 / 02 45
TELEX SET VIA CULLERCOATS RADIO
0715 BST Passing 2-8-93

Skippers Signature...... C J Ellis

VESSEL CATCH LOG BOOK
This page from the log book shows seven hauls on 1 August 1993 with the live weights of various fish caught by the *Christine Nielsen* under skipper Cliff Ellis

Fishing agent for the *Christine Nielsen* was Richard Irvin & Sons (of North Shields fish quay), who arranged for sales of the fish. The catches were mainly landed at North Shields, Esbjerg and Grimsby with occasional landings at Peterhead. Fishing areas mentioned in Cliff's log books include:

Yorkshire Dowsing to Inner Hole, Withernsea & Flamboro, East of Bayman's Scarp, Filey, Scarboro, Whitby Light, Pits, Red House, Well Edge, Long Harry's, South Lemon, Westward to Skaty, Scruffy, Haddock Bank, Smiths Knowle and Joiner Hole.

With further such evocative names as:
Sylt & White Bank, Middle Rough, Outer Rough, Inner Shoal, NW of Horn Reef LV, Bruces, Inner Hole, Coal Boat, Well Flat, Auk, Lisborgs Ridge, Devil's Holes, Helgoland and Clay Deeps.

In Cliff's small annual log books the column headers for hauls and catches indicate types of fish caught. Cliff decoded these for the author:

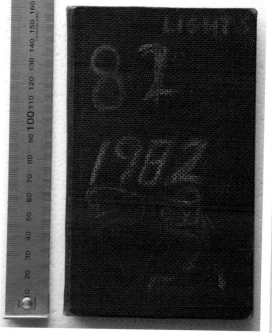

1200 BOXES OF FISH
Section of a page from Cliff's daily log book for 1982 indicating a record catch of fish, for the *Christine Nielsen*, worth £24,000 from one March fishing trip. T4.9+ relates to tides at the location on 26 March. Column headers 'FL – WT' are explained in the text; numbers below column headers indicate how many boxes of fish from each of two hauls

1982 LOG BOOK
Cliff's annual log book for 1982 (mm scale for size). He often purchased these note books from Harry Smith & Company in Nile Street, North Shields

- FL, FLS, PL (flatfish, plaice);
- LH (large haddock); DN (Danny's i.e. medium haddock); TD, TR (tiddlers i.e. small haddock);
- Sc (seconds i.e. best haddock, best size);
- LM (lemon sole);
- Mc (mediums i.e. codlings); SP (Sprag i.e. big cod – this is what they really sought!);
- WT (whiting);
- RB (Robbie i.e. tiny codlings, down to the limit of size allowed)
- RF (Ruff i.e. single / odd fish in their own boxes, for example a small shark)

Cliff fished throughout the year, but liked the fine weather of summer best. Winter produced the biggest catches and he'd often skipper his vessel for ten day trips in bad winter weather. With the *Christine Nielsen* he concentrated on catching fish, and would only catch odd boxes of prawns. To catch prawns in earnest the crew would need to change their boat's gear and use a finer mesh net. He would switch between trawling and seine net fishing as appropriate, describing seine net fishing as more difficult, but with potential to make larger catches than by trawling. Shooting a seine net and hauling would take about two hours, while if he was trawling the trawls lasted perhaps up to four hours or more. When fishing with a seine net he used 24 coils of rope, each coil of 120 fathoms, with 12 coils attached to each end of the net. Of his earlier fishing experiences from North Shields (1960s to mid-1970s) he said the main catches would be of flatfish, haddock, whiting and cod. Some prawns were also caught at that time, though not a lot, he told the author. When fishing in the west of the North Sea and steaming for North Shields after a trip, Cliff would radio ahead to Richard Irvin and pass information about the catch. He would only report catches on a daily basis if he was on the east side of the North Sea, as required by regulations when fishing in other waters – for example to the Norwegian fisheries people.

BRITISH EMPIRE MEDAL
Cliff Ellis was awarded the
B.E.M. in 1988 for services to fishing

BRITISH EMPIRE MEDAL
Obverse side

RECOMMENDATION LETTER
The Queen has approved the Prime Minister's
recommendation that Cliff should be awarded
with the British Empire Medal

10 DOWNING STREET
LONDON SW1A 2AA

From the Principal Private Secretary
IN CONFIDENCE

18 May 1988

Sir,

I have the honour to inform you that The Queen has been graciously pleased to approve the Prime Minister's recommendation that the British Empire Medal (B.E.M.) be awarded to you.

This award is due to be announced in the Birthday Honours List to be published on 11 June 1988; this letter must be treated as strictly confidential until then.

The award will be presented to you locally by the Lord-Lieutenant of your county or by a Minister of the Crown as The Queen's representative. Details of the time and place of the presentation will be sent to you in due course.

I should be glad if you would kindly complete the enclosed form and send it to me by return of post.

I am, Sir,
Your obedient Servant,

N. L. Wicks

C J Ellis Esq
72 Linskill Terrace
North Shields
Tyne & Wear

FEEDING THE GULLS
Cliff feeding the black-headed gulls beside the fish quay, 28 November 2010

Altogether Cliff spent 47 years at sea, retiring from the *Christine Nielsen* in 1998. He was awarded the British Empire Medal in June 1988 for "paying attention to the job" as he put it. Cliff had been recommended for the medal due to his contribution to fishing and for helping other fishermen. Other fishermen would ask him for advice, such as where to fish to make good catches, and many other things besides. He took an interest in the job and passed his knowledge on to others. He would talk to his crew aboard ship and received radio calls while at sea, from other fishing skippers – asking where he'd been and how to do this, that and the other. He advised young skippers and mentioned the friendly atmosphere when at sea. Cliff was presented with the medal by Sir Ralph Carr-Ellison (Lord Lieutenant of Tyne and Wear and area representative for the Royal Family) and received signed letters of congratulations from Neville Trotter (Member of Parliament for Tynemouth) and John MacGregor (Minister of Agriculture, Fisheries and Food). He has an associated letter on parchment from the Queen.

On 18 March 2001, after Cliff had retired, the *Christine Nielsen* flooded and sank 120 miles northeast of the river Tyne while trawling. The crew of three abandoned the vessel into the liferaft, from which they were rescued three hours later by a coastguard rescue helicopter.

Cliff has been married twice and has a son, daughters, step-daughters and grand-children. When his second wife died (in 1998) his family bought him Shep for company, a good-natured collie dog. For many years he enjoyed walking Shep in the river mouth and feeding the gulls and crows. Shep died in 2012 and is greatly missed by his master, but Cliff's family keep him occupied with their friendly visits. Cliff is a member of the local group of the Association of Retired Fishermen and attends their meetings and outings on a regular basis.

CLIFF AND TOMMY
Cliff Ellis B.E.M. (left) enjoys a joke with retired fisherman Tommy Bailey (senior) at the Low Lights car park, North Shields fish quay, 31 October 2010

CLIFF WITH SHEP
Cliff was Shep's master from 1998 to 2012. Photographed beside the fish quay sands, with the river entrance behind, 24 October 2010

Douglas Brunton Clark

Retired Cullercoats and North Shields fisherman (born 2 November 1923)

Doug and his family have a long association with the fishing industry in northeast England and many interesting stories to tell. Doug was born on 2nd November 1923 and went to Western School, North Shields, while the family lived in the town at No 2 Thrift Street (opposite what was then called the Pan / Pawn Shop Club i.e. Tynemouth Disabled and Ex-Servicemen's Club). At Western School Doug remembers the caretaker used to open up on some summer days so the children may go to play, since there was nothing much else for them to do. He also recalls that the train fare to Tynemouth from North Shields was then one old penny and often the residents of the whole street where he lived would get the train to Tynemouth and go on the Longsands. In 1934 he moved with his parents and grandmother to John Street, Cullercoats for a short period (possibly to the age of fourteen). The family then moved to a council house at Links Road (Cullercoats) where the rent was 17 shillings and 6 pence per week. In the early years of the Second World War Doug lived there with his parents and helped his mother part-time at their fish shop in Newcastle, when they had fish from Shields to sell; he also carried out some fishing. At North Shields fish quay they would be allocated a certain number of boxes of fish to collect, depending on how well the fishing was going, and their name would be called to collect the boxes – if they were not there they did not get the fish. Before they had

PORTRAIT
Seated at the Low Lights car park, North Shields fish quay, 16 August 2009. Behind are some of the buildings within Clifford's Fort

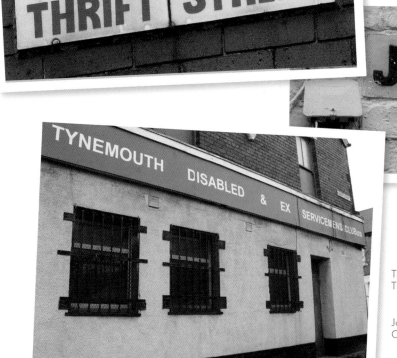

Thrift Street, name plate, North Shields. The Clark family lived at number 2

John Street, Cullercoats, name plate. The Clark family lived here for a short period

Pawn Shop Club, opposite the Clark's home in North Shields

the fish shop (where his mother paid rent of £10 per week) his mother used to sell fish on Nuns Lane, Newcastle, from her creel and basket – taking the train there from the coast. Doug recounts that within four to six weeks of the birth of each of her five children (three girls and two boys) their mother would carry a basket of fish, weighing four stones, to Newcastle to sell. His mother was called Mary and the police used to move her on when she was selling fish from her Nuns Lane creel. One of her customers asked her why the police kept moving her, and then took Mary to the police station. Here the lady spoke with her policeman husband, who was on duty, saying "Why do your men keep moving this lady on? If it wasn't for her we wouldn't have that nice fish every week!" From then onwards the police left Mary alone to sell her fish.

Doug's mother baited hooks for the fishermen at Cullercoats until she was 16 years old, then she went to work at Barry Noble's fruit shop in North Shields. She used to get paid one shilling for baiting 500 hooks with mussels. The mussels came by wagon. Sometimes her father and brother sailed to the river Tees for mussels – twice they beached their coble at Souter when caught in a storm. When she was aged sixteen an artist painted Mary at Cullercoats in her fisher clothes. Cullercoats had then become an attraction to artists, bringing for example …. John Falconer Slater, Robert Jobling and Winslow Homer. Doug recalled a local story that one visiting Cullercoats artist became friendly with a fisher girl so that her boyfriend broke off with her. This ex-boyfriend almost drowned when his boat capsized, but it seems the artist rescued him. The full intriguing story is recorded in Ron Wright's book (2002) where the artist is named as Henry Clouston, the year as 1831 and the fisher girl as Nanny Purvis. Doug's mother then sold fish in Gosforth, until her own mother died – when she took over her mother's sales position at Nuns Lane. Opposite where she stood at Nuns Lane was a butcher's shop above which was a fish and chippie. Later Mary took over the butcher's making it her own fish shop. "My mother was a very bold woman … there was not a picking on her!" Doug recalled. The Clark family

CULLERCOATS BAY PAINTING
Doug's mother and her father at Cullercoats Bay with swill baskets to hold coiled line and hooks.
A painting by Michael Smith

As a young lad. Photograph courtesy of Doug Clark

Nuns Lane, Newcastle. Doug's mother and grandmother sold fish here from a creel

29

have a creel made by Mary's father for her over a hundred years ago. Her father used to 'knit' salmon net. Doug's father, Andrew, was a foy boatman. He carried a long pole with a hook – he would go out in a coble and hook onto an incoming boat to help her berth on the river. Doug told that often the foy boatmen from north of the river Tyne would fight with the South Shields boatmen. His paternal grandfather ran a 'tangerine shop' which Doug said was a scrapyard … he would make purchases from ships.

In 1940 Doug was "shooting lines" from Cullercoats in a rowing boat with Tommy Giffy, who was also a glazier, and Andrew Cuddy, who also had a coble and used rowing boats both during and after the war. Andrew Cuddy would "shoot line" in the winter to catch fish (that is fishing with line and hook – perhaps 120 hooks with worm as bait). At times dead fish would float ashore all along the coast – killed by parachute mines dropped by the Germans during the war, the haddock and codling floated in the water. Doug recalled that one day a parachute mine exploded near Cullercoats and many dead fish were washed up.

Doug joined the Royal Air Force in 1941, trained as an air gunner and qualified as a deckhand gunman to become based, from 1942, at Wells-on-Sea, Norfolk, with 23 Squadron Air Sea Rescue for nearly two years. Flight Lieutenant Banner was remembered to be in command at first while Doug was based there, then after nearly two years a new Pilot Officer came into post and Doug applied to the parent station at RAF Bircham Newton (in west Norfolk) so he could be involved in trials of airborne lifeboats. So Doug transferred and was based at Bircham Newton for a further nine months or so. The early trials involved airborne lifeboats made from a type of neoprene, but these were not a great success. They were dropped from modified Lockheed Hudson bombers, but landed in the sea badly and generally folded on impact. Due to the poor success of the neoprene versions, yacht designer Uffa Fox came up with a very successful wooden framed airborne lifeboat which was dropped by parachute and fell at an angle of 30 degrees to land angled in the sea and as a consequence was not damaged. Naval architect W.T. (Bill) Waight advanced the design and implementation of the project. The first successful rescue with such a wooden-framed airborne lifeboat (in May 1943) was from Bircham Newton when the lifeboat was dropped from a Hudson to the crew of a Lancaster bomber who had ditched in the North Sea. Another Hudson circled as the lifeboat was dropped and the pilot and aircrew transferred from their Lancaster's rubber dingy (which inflated on hitting water), to the airborne lifeboat which had been dropped for them nearby.

The two Hudson aircraft returned to base at Wells-on-Sea while a Fairmile Class naval vessel from Grimsby sailed out to collect the ditched crew from their airborne lifeboat. Doug had hoped to be part of the RAF crew on a vessel from Wells-on-Sea, also taking the Hudson aircrew (who had dropped the lifeboat), to go out and pick up the Lancaster aircrew from the lifeboat, but they were overruled by the Navy which sent the vessel from Grimsby. Doug mentioned that Lancaster bombers had a good reputation for floating if they had ditched in the sea. 98 airborne lifeboats were dropped operationally, saving an estimated 200-300 lives.

AIRBORNE LIFEBOAT
World War II Mk 1 airborne lifeboat, Service No. Q III. The only known fully-restored example in the UK.
Photograph courtesy of Classic Boat Museum, East Cowes, Isle of Wight

Next Doug was sent by train to an airfield at Portreath on the west coast of Cornwall, where he arrived on base at eleven o'clock one evening in July 1944; a taxi was waiting to transfer him to the airfield when he arrived. He was told to find a bunk for the night and report for eight o'clock the next morning. That day he was flown to Cherbourg on a Lockheed Hudson aircraft while sitting beside an airborne lifeboat. He remained at Cherbourg for a few weeks where he helped man a crash tender – which attended to crashed aircraft at scattered airfields in the area. He recounted that the worst day he experienced here was when they attended to seven crashes, including two Flying Fortresses and a Mustang, at a small diversion airfield. The Fortresses took part in daylight raids and aircraft unable to return to their base would head for one of the diversion airfields which were just a field quickly prepared and fenced off with barbed wire. Doug recalled that the American aircrew here could buy a carton of cigarettes, a chocolate ration and chewing gum for one shilling and nine pence, but their lives could be counted in a matter of days as the missions were so dangerous.

After a few weeks he was in the French town of Amiens, where there had been a famous raid, when occupied by the Germans, by de Havilland Mosquitos to free resistance fighters from prisons. The Mosquitos dropped bombs to break the prison walls so the prisoners could be freed (258 prisoners escaped). Coincidence would have it that here Doug was tapped on the shoulder in the NAAFI by a chap he knew from home, the uncle of John Stocks (who fished from Cullercoats). From Amiens Doug moved to Belgium where he was based at two diversion airfields and later at an airfield from where Swordfish flew. The Swordfish were used, since they flew slowly, to track and bomb German midget submarines that were presumed to be in the area as ships started coming into Antwerp again. At Knokke in Belgium Doug met his wife-to-be, Lucienne, at a liberation dance. "This was the last place where the Germans held out at the end of the war," Doug said. On the day he met his future wife a liberation parade, with resistance fighters, had been held in the streets of Knokke. Lucienne's father had been in charge of the local resistance during the war and two of her cousins had been arrested by the Gestapo and vanished. Doug managed to wrestle with the administrative paper work and applied to his commanding officer before marrying on 12th May 1945. He had two days off to marry; there were two marriage ceremonies. "I had to get married twice", Doug said, once in the mayor's office (the official ceremony) and once in church the next day. War ended on 8th May 1945 at which point Doug had been away from home for two years and had some leave coming up, but he did not want to return home as he could not take his wife.

Anyway he returned to Northeast England on two weeks leave during which time he received an official telegram saying he was to go out to the Far East. However Doug ended up in Kirton Lyndsey, Lincolnshire, stacking equipment. He said he was "a bit of an agitator, trying to arrange his life as best he could while in the forces", and while based at Kirton Lyndsey a message came over the tannoy to summon him to report to the commanding officer. His mate wondered what he had been up to, but at this appointment he was told to report to Gatwick the next day as his wife was to be flown across from Belgium and he was to receive two weeks leave – his agitations had worked! On 4 July 1945 Lucienne was flown to England and the war in the Far East had almost finished, so Doug was not needed there. On her arrival, by train, at Newcastle, the groom's family were present to inspect his wife. On Tyneside Lucienne lived with Doug's mother and in Sept 1945 he left the RAF on compassionate leave and was able to return to help run his mother's fish shop in Newcastle.

WEDDING DAY
Doug and Lucienne in church, Belgium, May 1945.
Photographs courtesy of Doug Clark

Lucienne spoke English from the age of eleven. She used to help her aunt in her beach café where often English folk would visit while on holiday, later progressing to work in a fish shop. Towards the end of the war Doug was stationed at a hotel (on the Belgian coast) and had walked to a coastal café with an RAF friend. Here they were told that there was to be a Liberation dance that night. "I had never been to a dance before," said Doug, so they decided to go. At the dance Doug met Lucienne and she soon realised this was the man she would marry. She broke off an engagement with a Belgian lad to pair up with Doug. The second marriage ceremony was held in a Catholic church almost a mile from Lucienne's family home – the wedding party walked there and back. Lucienne's cousin made a wedding cake, while the best man was Doug's corporal. Doug's mother had previously posted an engagement ring to her son, which he had paid for.

Originally Doug had been going to join the Merchant Navy during the Second World War. He used to hang around with six of his mates around Past Times, an amusement arcade by the Spanish City (Whitley Bay) which Doug said "was always busy during the war with soldiers." However when Doug witnessed a Swedish steam merchant ship called *Mars* blow up when leaving Blyth this put him off that course and his path diverged as outlined earlier. *Mars* struck a mine, laid by U-boat U-22, on 20 December 1939 and she sank one mile east of the St. Marys light vessel – seven died and fifteen survived. "You had to be seventeen to join the Merchant Navy," Doug explained, and he was still too young at this time. Of his six friends, four were lost on the same ship on their first trip in the Merchant Navy during the war, another was later lost during the war while serving in the Merchant Navy, while the sixth (Doug's best friend – Larry Barnes) was killed (along with his sister and mother) at Garden Square, Cullercoats when a bomb landed beside the boat yard. It appears the German aircraft had been attempting to hit the wireless station at Marconi Point, Cullercoats (this incident seems to have been on 5/6 May 1941, Mon/Tue, midnight to 3.00 a.m., 3 people were reported to have died at Cullercoats).

As previously mentioned Doug's maternal grandmother used to stand and sell fish in Nuns Lane, Newcastle, in front of a butcher's shop. When his grandmother died his mother continued this practice eventually running a stall in the open fish market at Newcastle. At times Doug's eldest sister and brother also worked there. When Doug joined the air force he earned about ten shillings a week, but after the war, when he worked at the family fish shop, he was earning seven pounds a week. Many of the men Doug served with in the RAF were Irish. Even though he remembered the low forces pay, an Irish PT instructor told him of being better paid in the RAF than when bus driving in Southern Ireland. Lucienne got a job sewing dresses for a tailor and earned three pounds a week while Doug worked at the fish shop. The family fish shop closed in 1956.

Before and after World War II colliers loaded their cargo at the staithes on the river Tyne. Some coal would fall into the river, so when dredgers cleaned the river this spilled coal would be dumped three miles out to sea. "In winter gales from the south east some of this coal would wash ashore in front of St George's Church," Doug recalled. "It was knee high on the beach and many locals would come to gather it. The coal was slightly rounded and flattened by the sea."

Before their fish shop closed Doug had started earning a living as a fisherman straight after the war, initially part-time. He firstly bought a rowing boat for ten pounds, followed later by a second rowing boat which he had moored off the South Pier at Cullercoats. Then he bought *Jenny*, an eighteen foot double-headed coble with an Austin seven car engine which he used for hauling lobster pots. One day *Jenny* caught fire while next to Marconi Point (Cullercoats) so Davy Taylor and Jacky Gibson launched a rowing boat to come and help him put out the fire using a bucket. A good friend of Doug, Jacky Gibson went down to work in the coal mines in Kent, but was killed in a car accident when returning to the northeast to attend his daughter's wedding.

ALPHA
Cobles *Alpha* (right) and *Challenge*, North Shields fish quay, 22 May 2010. *Alpha* was built at Cullercoats by Peter Fairbairn assisted by Doug Clark

Fisherman Peter Fairbairn (whose daughter married Doug's son Dennis) used some of the wood remaining from *Jenny*, along with some wood he bought from Blyth, to build a new coble at Cullercoats … called *Alpha*. Doug stated that, "*Alpha* is the only coble ever built at Cullercoats" and went on to say that this boat had returned to the Cullercoats boat yard in late 2009. Doug helped Peter to build *Alpha* in an old cottage which was underground – and he recalls there were one or two shops above it. The coble was built at 26 feet in length while the room they used was only 27 feet long. Initially she had an old car engine fitted, but on the launch they could not get the engine started. Doug did some sea trout fishing with Peter Fairbairn in *Alpha* at St Mary's Island – they would shoot a net at night. After *Jenny*, Peter owned the coble *Sunbeam* which was nearly lost on one occasion. Doug fished with Geordie Armstrong in *Sunbeam* and one day they were out from Cullercoats in a big swell and had hauled the pots, but thick fog developed. They were looking for the entrance to Cullercoats harbour and were just south of the harbour, off South Crab Hill rocks, east from St George's Church. The boat was washed onto and over these rocks losing the rudder while the propeller grated over the rocks, and they were washed into Slaty Gut (just down from St George's Church), the boat almost went over and they were left with two oars as a means of propulsion. They were "very lucky," Doug said. They "fetched her astern and put the anchor down" and started to bale her out. Fortunately they were towed into Cullercoats harbour and later their rudder and tiller were picked up from Tynemouth beach. Peter Fairbairn later went on to fish with large trawlers.

ST GEORGE'S CHURCH
North end of Tynemouth Longsands with St George's Church, the village of Cullercoats and Brown's (or Marconi) Point. With frost on the shore, 23 November 2008

Peter Fairbairn's father, Norman, had been at Dunkirk in the Second World War and was captured by the German troops and put in a hospital in Ghent having been hit in the head by a bullet. Austrian surgeons carried out a delicate operation on Norman which included patching his head wound with silver. In 1943 Norman was repatriated during an exchange of badly wounded soldiers. Doug mentioned Norman was bothered for the rest of his life by this head wound.

In 1956 Doug had a double-headed fully decked-in boat built at Seahouses – she was called *Margaret and Dennis,* named after his daughter and son. She was built at a cost of £2,500 with the help of a grant and loan leaving Doug to pay off his share in instalments of three pounds per week, if he could afford it – as he had two young children. His wife was also working part-time as a waitress at the Park Hotel (Tynemouth) at this time to help pay the bills and they took in two lodgers for thirty shillings each a week. He often worked this keelboat down as far as Sunderland with lobster pots and then he went on to use long-lines in winter with worm, catching codlings. They would fish with three lines of 400 hooks with black worm as bait – this came from Norfolk at a cost of £4.50 for 1,200 delivered worms (ordered the previous

MARGARET AND DENNIS
Built at Seahouses in 1956. Painting by Douglas Rutter of Seahouses

day for a 10 a.m. delivery). They fished for codlings near the wreck of *Oslofjord* south of the Tyne south pier. Norwegian passenger ship *Oslofjord* (converted to a troop ship) was beached at South Shields due to hitting a German acoustic mine when going towards the Tyne on 1 December 1940 – there was one casualty from this incident. A Greek steamer *Eugenia Chandris* ran into the *Oslofjord* wreck later off South Shields (15 March 1943) causing her to sink alongside and atop her.

Doug said fishing was tough at this time and the fishermen made their own gear (lobster pots, etc). In 1965 when out fishing with the *Margaret and Dennis* on one occasion there was thick snow when Doug and his mate Jo had 54 stones of crab on board and one lobster, "we tossed a coin for the lobster!" Due to the weight of the catch the boat was low in the gunnels. Their buyer purchased the crab for four shillings a stone and sold them at twelve shillings a stone, making a handsome profit, but not for Doug! Doug stated "No matter how hard you worked you were getting no further ahead in the winter". Three divers once hired the *Margaret and Dennis* for a fee of £10 a day. They dived at the wreck of the cargo steam ship *Rio Colorado*, built in Sunderland, sunk by a German submarine mine off the Tyne in March 1917

MARGARET CLARK
Built at Seahouses in 1965-67. Painting by Douglas Rutter of Seahouses

while carrying a cargo of wheat. Doug's mother had witnessed the sinking and he was given the ship's telegraph by the divers.

Next *Margaret Clark,* a trawler, was built for Doug at Seahouses in 1965-67 at a cost of £12,500 and he made regular payments of £16 per week. The older *Margaret and Dennis* fishing boat was sold to provide a deposit for this new vessel. Doug's mate Joe, who'd been on minesweepers in WWII and had already been a skipper on trawlers, was very useful when it came to Doug's new boat. They fished together from North Shields on *Margaret Clark* for fish and prawns. Such work was not without mishap. One day Doug had a narrow escape when his jumper caught in the winch drive down below decks when the trawler was in Shields harbour. His son Dennis quickly switched off the winding gear and the rescuers had to cut off his jumper to release him. Fortunately injury had been averted, but the jumper had been pulled tight like a tourniquet on Doug's arm. The crew of the *Sovereign* came to Doug's rescue that day. On another occasion a hydraulic pipe burst aboard and severely

PARACHUTE MINE
Dennis Clark sitting astride parachute mine aboard the *Margaret Clark*.
Photograph courtesy of Doug Clark

TALLY
Margaret Clark tally – used to mark boxes of fish for the market

cut his right hand. A subsequent accident aboard involved his son Dennis's hand becoming caught in the net drum. On another occasion a door aboard slammed on Doug's left hand cutting off the tips of his middle three fingers. These finger tips were saved and sewn back into place quite neatly at hospital! One day aboard *Margaret Clark*, when son Dennis was aged about 17, they winched aboard their net to find it held what Joe thought was the wing from an early jet plane – and they let it thud to the deck. However they soon found out what it was – a Second World War parachute mine. They left it off South Shields for the naval disposal men from Rosyth to deal with. The team used a local police launch and exploded the mine offshore, but the explosion and wash "nearly half filled the police launch with water." Later the buoy, marking the spot to leave such items, was moved from South Shields to off St Mary's Island where there are no nearby homes in which windows may shatter during such explosions of armaments.

In 1979 a boat designer called Dennis Squires came from Cornwall and designed the vessel *Luc* for Doug. Mr Crutwell built small boats at the Tyne Brand site at the fish quay and he got a shed upriver with two cranes to build *Luc*. A large deposit was paid to Mr Crutwell in August 1979 to build the boat which should have been ready and fishing by February 1980, but the costs increased rapidly. There were delays and in July 1981 the vessel was towed away to be completed by the Clark family themselves by February 1982, delayed two years from the original plan. The *Margaret Clark* was sold to cover part of the bank loan. *Luc* was subsequently nearly lost twice at sea through filling with water "when she sucked in instead of pumping out". The vessel is still fishing from North Shields, and after Doug retired as skipper of the *Luc*, he was followed in this role by his son Dennis and then his grandson Peter. The boat was named after Doug's Belgian nephew – his wife's sister's son, whose father was in charge of the brickworks where he worked. Luc died at the age of 21, two days after an accident at work. Doug attended the large funeral in Belgium.

Doug had a cousin, Robert Brunton, who was coxswain with the Tynemouth lifeboat *Tynesider* from 1 February 1963 to 30 November 1976. He had served on minesweepers with the Royal Naval Patrol Service (RNPS) during the Second World War and was awarded the DSM (Distinguished Service Medal) in 1941, in recognition of his service in the 1916, Auxiliary Patrol trawler, HM Trawler *Norland* during air attacks on 26-27 July 1941 and 4 August 1941. Seaman Robert was presented with his decoration at an Investiture held on 5 May 1942. Robert was also second coxswain of the Tynemouth lifeboat from 1953 to 1963 having commenced as a

LUC (SN 36)
Fishing vessel *Luc* is returning to port, passing South Shields Groyne and the government jetty, 26 February 2011.
Built on the Tyne for Doug Clark, 1979 - 1982

lifeboatman in 1948. He was involved as a crew member in one of the longest rescues in Tynemouth's history to date, which involved a German ship *MV* (Motor Vessel) *Hans Hoth* (370 tons, with a crew of nine) on which the cargo of coal had shifted in heavy seas. This resulted in her developing a list of 35 degrees on her journey

THREE GENERATIONS
From left: Peter, Dennis and Doug Clark with *Luc* in the background, North Shields fish quay, 2 May 2009

from Barrowstounness (Bo'ness, West Lothian), in the Firth of Forth, to Hamburg. The lifeboat was launched on the Tyne at 12.15 p.m. on 9 February 1952 reaching *Hans Hoth* at 00.38 a.m. on 10 February, around 81 miles NE of the Tyne (according to the last position provided by an RAF Shackleton aircraft at 22:43 hours, on a bearing of 56 degrees from the Tyne). The lifeboat stood by the ship for two hours before returning to the Tyne – arriving back to moor at 9.55 p.m. after experiencing very bad weather for 33 hours and 40 minutes. *Hans Hoth* was taken in tow by tug *Hendon*, but sank some 16 miles off the Tyne with no loss of life, since the tug had taken off her crew. When Tynemouth lifeboat *Tynesider* returned from this service she was very low on fuel. In addition other stores required replenishment – oil, flares, bully beef, biscuits, soup, cocoa milk, chocolate and two bottles of rum!

Note. In the famous (and considerably longer) Daunt Rock light-vessel *Comet* (gold medal) RNLI service of 1936, the Ballycotton crew (on Barnet class lifeboat the *Mary Stanford,* ON733) only had three hours' sleep in 63 hours out on service with a total of 49 hours at sea. The crew of eight were saved from the light-vessel during terrible conditions.

Eileen McConnell

Tynemouth resident who cared for sick, injured and abandoned birds, with interests in local & visiting wildlife and river shipping movements

Barbara Frances Eileen McConnell, (née Robson) was born in 1926 in Whitburn (Tyne and Wear), her mother Muriel (née Martin) was from the river Tees area and her father (Frank Robson) originated from Newcastle, but neither was "into wildlife". Eileen mentioned her father was involved in shipping on Teeside. She went to boarding school at Casterton, near Kirkby Lonsdale (Cumbria) from the age of 13 (in 1939) to 17 and then attended Mrs Hoster's Secretarial College in London which was evacuated, during the war, to Stamford in Lincolnshire. A year followed during which she worked as a secretary at the Ministry of Information in Newcastle and, after leaving this job (around 1946) she spent a year in London with the German section of the British Foreign Office. Next came Germany, arriving in 1947, working for the Control Commission for Germany – British Element, as part of the Allied occupation – when she had many dealings with the Germans and worked as a secretary attending conferences, etc. She had learnt German at school, but was a secretary rather than an interpreter. Returning from Germany at the end of 1949 Eileen took up employment with an American sporting author (A H Higginson) in Dorset and she helped with a book on which he was working. Higginson was a master of two packs of hounds in Dorset and his father had founded the Boston Symphony Orchestra. She used her shorthand and typing skills to assist with the book and also sorted out the wages for her employer's household servants, who numbered between seven and fifteen. Eileen recalls that Higginson also wrote articles for *The Field* country magazine.

Higginson A H, 1951. An Old Sportsman's Memories 1876 - 1951 An Autobiography by Alexander Henry Higginson. Blue Ridge Press, Berryville, Virginia.

Eileen left her Dorset employment in 1950, before completion of the book, to return north, as her father was ill. At first she lived at the YWCA (Young Women's Christian Association) in Newcastle, until her father died in 1952, and then moved to live in a flat at Percy Gardens, Tynemouth, with her mother. From 1950-58 she was employed at King's College, Newcastle (which was part of Durham University) as secretary to the college registrar. A neighbouring resident at Percy Gardens was Maurice F. McConnell and his family ... they met and became friends.

Eileen and Maurice married in 1958 and the couple moved into The Old House, 45 Front Street, Tynemouth where they lived for the next 25 years until 1983. Here Eileen

KITTIWAKE
Kittiwake adult, North Shields Fish Quay, 8 June 2013

took to looking after sick, injured and oiled birds which were brought to her for care. Husband Maurice worked for Newcastle Breweries, where he was in charge of wines and spirits and was also a director, and he "just went with it" when Eileen took to caring for birds at their home.

Maurice's father Dr James McConnell M.B., M.R.C.S., D.P.H. (who died in 1948) was school medical officer for the County Borough of Tynemouth (i.e. including North Shields) for 34 years from the inception of this work in the Borough in September or October 1908 to his retirement on 8 February 1943. James and his family had lived in Percy Gardens, Tynemouth, since the late nineteenth century. Maurice's uncle Alexander (Alec) McConnell, Chairman of Newcastle Breweries, had bought The Old House, Front Street, Tynemouth just before World War II. The rear of the property was badly damaged when a land mine exploded in the castle moat during the war, so Alexander did not move in until after the war by

OLD HOUSE
The Old House, Front Street, Tynemouth, 27 April 2012

which time his wife, Ethel, had died. In the house deeds, and elsewhere, it is recorded that The Old House was built (in 1756) by a bricklayer, William Haxton and his son-in-law George Anderson, on the site of a property purchased by Haxton from William Collinson of Tynemouth. The house deeds show in June 1762 that George Anderson sold the property to 'master and mariner' Robert Bland for the sum of £315. When Uncle Alec died in 1958, Maurice and Eileen bought The Old House together. Another relation of Maurice, Mr John Arnot Williamson, was Honorary Secretary of Tynemouth Volunteer Life Brigade (T.V.L.B.) from 1916 - 1950, previously joint Hon Sec from 1906 - 1916 with Mr J.J. Howard Catcheside until the latter's death. John Williamson was presented with the M.B.E. by His Majesty King George VI for his services in connection with the Tynemouth Volunteer Life Brigade, in total a member for sixty seven years. In October 1955, Mr D. A. Williamson, John's son, was invited to become President of the T.V.L.B., which he accepted, continuing until his death in June 1963. Eileen's husband was also a member of the T.V.L.B. and Hon Sec from July 1957 until he passed away early in 1995. He was also appointed Honorary Captain of the Brigade in 1960. In December 1932 Dr James McConnell (Maurice's father) was appointed Honorary Medical Officer of the T.V.L.B. a position from which he resigned in September 1946. James's father was a William McConnell who, at the time of the 1881 census, was aged 51 and living at 25 Percy Gardens, Tynemouth. The census recorded William as a ship owner, married to Hannah (then aged 41) and son James was then aged 3 years. Although the census records him as a ship owner, Eileen believes he was instead involved with the breweries. William McConnell was a regular attender at the Congregational Church in Front Street and died on 8 January 1900 with internment at Preston Cemetery. Maurice McConnell's Uncle William, son of William the 'ship owner', tragically drowned with a friend off

WATCH HOUSE
Home of the TVLB. The Watch House, Spanish Battery, Tynemouth, 3 January 2014

MAURICE MCCONNELL
Maurice F McConnell (left), Councillor John Spence (Mayor, centre) and Captain William G Hunter. Presentation of model lifesaving hand cart on Friday 4 December 1964 at TVLB Centenary at Bath Assembly Rooms, Tynemouth. Photograph by courtesy of TVLB

Blyth on 24 June 1900. The Shields Daily News of Monday 25 June 1900 reports on the incident. William, aged 28 years, had left Tynemouth Haven in a small sailing canoe (named *Deuchar*) with the owner, Mr J Bell, a neighbour from No 32 Percy Gardens. They left in fine weather and proceeded to Blyth, which they reached and where they went ashore, leaving on their return journey in the afternoon. A heavy rainstorm then occurred and the two were 'thrown into the sea' just outside Blyth Harbour. The newspaper article states 'Both gentlemen were very well known in the neighbourhood, and were not inexperienced yachtsmen.'

When living at The Old House, Eileen and Maurice had four or five rescue dogs which they exercised beside Admiral Lord Collingwood's monument, overlooking the river – and they also had some cats. James Fisher (whose mother was a McConnell), well known ornithologist and author of many books on birds (see examples below), was a cousin of Maurice McConnell.

Examples of books by James Fisher (cousin of Maurice McConnell):
- *Birds as Animals*, 1939, W Heinemann
- *Watching birds*, 1941, Penguin Books, paperback
- *Bird Recognition*, *Volumes One and Two*, 1947, Penguin Books, paperback
- *The Fulmar*, 1952, Collins
- *The Shell Bird Book*, 1966, Ebury Press and Michael Joseph
- *Shell Nature Lovers' Atlas*, 1966, Ebury Press and Michael Joseph
- *Birds: an introduction to ornithology*, 1971, Aldus Books, posthumously with Roger Tory Peterson.

Eileen's records show that in the period 1962 to 1976, while caring for sick, injured, abandoned and rescued birds at The Old House she dealt with at least 2,272 birds of around 90 different species. 81% of the total comprised just eleven species, while there were single occurrences for 32 species. The species handled most of all was the guillemot, with at least 433 recorded. Of the guillemots 155 oiled individuals occurred between July 1975 and June 1976. In a newspaper cutting (Evening Chronicle) from 23 March 1970 it was noted she needed nearly 60 lbs of fresh fish every week to feed her birds. In dealing with oiled seabirds Eileen assisted the Research Unit on the Rehabilitation of Oiled Seabirds of Newcastle University, which was directed by Prof John Croxall from 1972 to 1975. She handled at least 572 gulls of seven different species ... mostly herring gull and kittiwake, dealing with many young birds during

Guillemot, Colonsay, 22 May 2007.
© Ian Fisher

Glaucous Gull first-winter, N Shields Fish Quay,
4 December 2013

Gannet adult, Bass Rock, East Lothian,
29 August 2013

the breeding season. The rarest gull she handled was a glaucous gull, this species nests in Iceland. Her bird was an immature found at North Shields fish quay on 23 March 1973. The gull died that night and was handed to the Hancock Museum collection in Newcastle. Eileen dealt with over two hundred each of homing (or feral) pigeons, blackbirds and house sparrows with a further 125 starlings. Birds of prey comprised 42 individuals of seven species, including four types of owl: little, tawny, barn and short-eared. Wading birds she handled comprised 15 species, including single ringed plover, sanderling, jack snipe, common snipe, bar-tailed godwit and water rail. Other species included five types of duck and thrush, four auk species, two red-throated divers, four storm petrels, two arctic skuas, one great skua and a dozen fulmars. Various song and perching birds that passed through her hands included finches, a meadow pipit and robin, black redstart, blue tit and likely four species of warbler. The crow family featured well with 24 rooks, 19 jackdaws, five carrion crows and a quartet of magpies. Eileen would give names to some birds and, although many died soon after being handed in and others were put to sleep, those that recovered were released back into the wild or handed for care to other collections. The author recalls, as a teenager, handing several birds found on local beaches to Eileen, including guillemots, a kittiwake and juvenile gannet.

Tales from a few of Eileen's birds follow. An adult swallow was found on 30 May 1971 aboard a seine-netter from North Shields, was handed to Eileen and died later from a haemorrhage. An adult oystercatcher was given to Eileen on 15 April 1968 by the police – it had been found near North Shields fish quay. This wading bird had an overgrown and curved beak (it should have been straight), was hand-fed by Eileen

Jackdaw, Killingworth, 12 April 2008.
© Ian Fisher

Fulmar, Old Hartley, 6 June 2007

Mallard duck, Tynemouth boating lake,
5 January 2014

and died almost seven years later on 18 January 1975. A woodpigeon was handed over on 5 May 1967 covered in soot. It was washed and released in Preston on 17 June 1967. The lady who handed in this pigeon was called Mrs Bulman – who worked for the RSPCA. A juvenile merlin, with right wing slightly drooping, was handed to Eileen on 25 August 1968. This small falcon was passed to Northumbrian wildlife artist James Alder on 13 September and it died in December of the same year. A jackdaw handed in by the RSPCA on 3 September 1965 was named 'Jackie 1' by Eileen. It had a lump removed from its foot on 6 September. This bird escaped on 8 June, but returned very hungry the next day. 'Jackie 1' was kept in captivity for a further six years until dying on 24 August 1971. A juvenile fulmar found on 31 August 1968 at Marsden was handed in and later released on 15 September when it flew off high. Eileen's brief diagnosis on this seabird was 'Probably too fat?' A mallard was found hiding in the cliffs near St Mary's Island on 9 January 1967, cold and exhausted. Eileen named the duck 'Cliff' and fed it on wheat in a bowl of water. It was released some five weeks later at [Old] Hartley on 12 February – flocks of mallards were said to be on the sea nearby. A badly oiled adult cormorant, found at the Tynemouth pier rocks on 17 April 1967, had been

Blackbird, Big Waters Nature Reserve (Brunswick Village), 19 February 2008. © Ian Fisher

Little Auk (mounted) in the snow, N Shields Fish Quay, 18 January 2013 ringed, on the right leg, at the Farne Islands on 16 July 1963. It was released at the Black Middens on 8 August 1967 and later seen swimming and diving. Some of the injuries recorded for her 1968 blackbirds include: molested by a cat, flew into window, legs paralysed, damaged upper mandible and car accident. A juvenile cuckoo found at Percy Gardens, Tynemouth, on 18 August 1968 had no tail – it died three days later on 21st. One of two little auks found in December 1970 was fed on small sprats, but it died of pneumonia on 19 January 1971. Another little auk was found at the Esso Terminal at North Shields on 13 February 1969, where it had likely been storm driven, but it died during the night. An adult guillemot found on 31 October 1967 by fisherman Mr Morse went very lame and became crippled. It was put to sleep on 12 February 1968. 'Laddie', a guillemot from near Tynemouth pier, was found on 13 December 1966 in summer plumage and died on 14 August 1967. Another delightful newspaper cutting, from page 7 of the Shields Weekly News edition on 24 December 1965, records a few tales of Eileen's bird patients, including the jackdaw which would step into the house kitchen from an outdoor garden aviary to locate his 'toy' – a shining florin.

WITH PIGEONS
Feeding the feral pigeons, Low Lights car park, 2 September 2007

In 1983 Maurice and Eileen moved along Front Street, to number 55, beside the vet (Strachan, Tyson & Hamilton). At their new address there was not enough room to care for birds, so Eileen gave this up and continued her daily walks to North Shields Fish Quay and Tynemouth Haven. Maurice died in January 1995 and Eileen moved from Front Street in 2004, but remains a Tynemouth resident.

Walking to the fish quay Eileen feeds the gulls, pigeons and crows (a recent addition to our river mouth avian flora) – mostly with wheat. Her walks, often in the afternoon, are curtailed in icy conditions, otherwise she ventures out in various weather.

Eileen mentioned (to the author) seeing an interesting herring gull at the Low Lights car park from June 2011. The author later observed the bird and continued to watch it several times between July and 2 October, when it was last seen. This was a first-summer bird (i.e. one year old) and was unusual in the fact that the upper mandible was perhaps 3-4 centimetres longer than it ought to be and curved downwards. It seemed able to look after itself and was observed eating chips thrown by visitors to the car park. Eileen named this individual 'Beaky' and it was a regular inhabitant of the river mouth for a few months.

BEAKY
Herring Gull 'Beaky',
Low Lights car park,
23 July 2011

An interest in the shipping movements on the river prompted Eileen to purchase a radio (in 2009) to monitor the transmissions to and from the ships so she could learn more about such traffic and know when to expect particular passing ships. Leonard Park, retired ship's captain and Tynemouth lifeboat volunteer, helped Eileen learn how to use the radio. She often hears the staff from the Port of Tyne, including the harbour masters, communications officers and river pilots over the radio. This prompted a visit to the harbour master control room at North Shields west quay to meet some staff, tour their office, talk with them and find out how they work.

WITH LEONARD PARK
Sitting beside Captain Leonard Park adjusting shipping radio, Low Lights car park, 17 May 2009

DAWN CORMORANTS
Just before sunrise on Sunday, 11 November 2012. Cormorants stand at the end of Lloyd's jetty in the cool morning air

Jackie Weatherstone

Retired North Shields seaman and fisherman (born 26 January 1935)

Jackie was born at home in Tyne Street (North Shields), overlooking the Haddock Shop dry dock on the riverside below. His dad was a riveter on the Tyne at the Swan Hunter shipyard who spent World War II working at Southampton docks. Jackie joined the Merchant Navy at the age of sixteen, spending around eighteen years as a merchant seaman. During this time he worked mostly deep sea on "tramps" and oil tankers, travelling five times round the world and passing through the Suez Canal to return via the Panama Canal. He spent a six month season off the Australian coast, and another season at the Great Lakes of Canada carrying grain to Montreal through the Saint Lawrence Seaway. These jobs were obtained mostly through the labour pool at South Shields and generally involved sailing from the Tyne, but also from Glasgow and London. For two years, in the winters of 1965 - 1967, he worked on colliers plying from the river Tyne to the river Thames and with them would travel to Battersea Power Station passing the Houses of Parliament. In the early 1960's Jackie was working on cargo ships of the Whalton Shipping Company Ltd, based in Newcastle, which owned four or five ships. He would go on trips that lasted between twelve and eighteen months at a time (nowadays such trips are limited to six months before the crew are allowed to fly home for a break).

PORTRAIT
At the fish quay, 25 May 2012

In 1960 he was on a ship called the *Reaveley* travelling between India and Japan. Nearing Japan, he was on deck when some rough weather struck. While on the starboard outer deck he heard the heavy sea approaching and was washed from the starboard to the port side and hit his back and side on the deck and hatches as he went. The skipper had just shouted that he was going to alter course as the heavy sea approached and Jackie, at that point, lost his footing as the sea hit. If there had been railings around the edge of the deck he would have been washed through and overboard, but there was a steel superstructure which saved him being washed into the sea and he grabbed hold of a safety rope as he was washed across the deck. He damaged and broke a bone in his leg, broke another in his hand and chipped a third bone in his back. His hand swelled and his back was very painful. The *Reaveley* was built on the Tyne by Swan Hunter & Wigham Richardson Ltd at their Neptune Yard, Low Walker. She was launched in September 1955.

REAVELEY
The *Reaveley* in 1956. Built on the Tyne by Swan Hunter & Wigham Richardson and launched in September 1955. Photograph courtesy of the Clive Ketley Collection

From Japan the ship went on to Australia then through the Panama Canal to Saint John, New Brunswick. At Saint John Jackie visited a Blue Cross hospital, dealing with army and navy casualties, and they determined that he needed treatment on his back and that his leg had healed itself. Jackie opted to have his back dealt with in the UK, however the skipper of the vessel would not allow him to fly home, so he needed to travel with the cargo ship which was now bound for the Mediterranean, working at washing onboard as he travelled. However the vessel was diverted to Hull and, on arrival at home, he was placed in a plaster body cast. He was no better after six months and then admitted to Tynemouth Victoria Jubilee Infirmary in North Shields (Hawkey's Lane) for six weeks while he had an operation. This involved the removal of damaged bone and a disc from his back and the fusion of two of his vertebrae. An eighteen inch scar on his back was held together by twenty two clips, and he was disabled for a year after the operation. He was told that only about forty percent of people who underwent such an operation were able to work afterwards. Nowadays such treatment would be dealt with through less invasive keyhole surgery. Jackie was told he would be twenty percent disabled for the rest of his life and in 1964

HANDS AND NET
Jackie is busy with a fishing net, North Shields fish quay, 1 September 2012

was paid off from the cargo company with a payment of £300, thus ending his period with deep sea cargo vessels. He has worked ever since, but has not received any disability payments.

In 1964 T. R. Dowson & Co Ltd, a shipyard at Tyne Dock (South Shields), had a sale as they were going out of business. Jackie bought a 42 foot launch called the *T J Dowson*, for £700 plus 5% commission. She was later renamed to *Sea Fisher*. This boat had a large petrol / diesel Kelvin J4, 44 horsepower engine in which the diesel would dirty the spark plugs which needed daily cleaning. In 1965 he bought a new and smaller engine, a Perkins 4.236 running at 90 horsepower. The Kelvin engine had become "knackered" after six months of service. This new engine with gearbox cost Jackie £360, but he said such an engine nowadays would be priced around £7,000 excluding gearbox. He travelled to a boat show in London to purchase the Perkins. Patterson's at South Shields fitted the engine which enabled the launch to travel at nine knots. Around this time Jackie also bought an ex Tyne customs launch,

which he renamed to *Sea Cat*. This launch still carried two bullet holes in the thick and heavy glass of the front window, reminders of its war service. The *Sea Cat* had a six cylinder Thornycroft marine diesel engine and a forward wheelhouse. She was approximately 26 feet in length and carvel-built (i.e. with a smooth hull). He also purchased the *Magnet* which was built in the Haven at Tynemouth by either a Mr Fry of Cullercoats or another party (other than Geordie Scott). George (or Geordie) Scott used to have a coble called *Linda Scott* and was married to Annie Dick, sister of local fisherman Albert Dick. Geoff Nugent (Michael's father) used to fish for salmon with Geordie Scott and Oliver (Ollie) Tweedy on this coble. Each of Jackie's three boats was used to take fishing parties offshore from the Tyne seven days a week, at one time charging ten shillings per person per day. Once a month he would take the local chief constable (from Morpeth) out fishing accompanied by sufficient drink to make for a happy trip.

In the summers of 1965 - 1967 he fished for salmon with Albert Dick. Then in 1968 Jackie got his own salmon license and fished from his boat *Sea Fisher*. Monofilament line had just come onto the scene and Jackie drove his VW beetle car from North Shields to Aberdeen and back in a day to collect some monofilament net. In 1968 he had an excellent season catching 200 to 300 fish each day, with sea trout for sale at about two shillings a pound and salmon at five to six shillings (or more) a pound. When salmon fishing off South Shields beach he used a 'J' net into which the salmon would swim. He used to call the area around the back of the south pier the 'playground' where good catches could be made many years ago and this continues even today. There are now only a handful of salmon boats left fishing in Northumberland, Durham and Teeside, compared to almost 300 in years gone by. He said that in 1968 he often went out fishing on a Friday morning to return by noon of the following day; this was the stipulated time to cease salmon fishing on a Saturday.

1970 was also a good fishing year for Jackie, but one day his engine overheated and he lost a week's work. However the chap who bought the fish from Jackie, Jimmy Hill who was based up Tanners Bank, said he would pay for a new engine for him, since he was having such a successful time at sea. However Jackie said he didn't need a new engine, as the one he had was already quite new, but he did say he would like a new boat! So Jimmy Hill agreed to help fund this venture.

So, in the winter of 1970 - 1971 Jackie sold his three boats: *Sea Fisher*, *Sea Cat* and *Magnet* and went looking for a seine-net fishing vessel. He bought the *Karen Obbekaer* (built 1945 in Denmark) in 1971 from Newlyn and sailed her to North Shields. She had a 150 horsepower Gleniffer V8 (eight cylinder) engine. In 1963 Gleniffer (of Anniesland, in Glasgow) was taken over by Kelvin, another Glasgow engine building company. Jimmy Hill set up a company called Karen Fishing Co Ltd, and both he and Jackie each put in £3,000. They borrowed a further £6,000 from

MAKING HAY NET
Jackie makes a horse's hay net at the fish quay, 12 August 2012

the bank. The boat cost £6,000, and a further £3,000 was used to rig out the vessel for fishing. Jackie worked *Karen Obbekaer* (BCK 134) from North Shields until early in the 1990s. Local fisherman Roy Elliott, a neighbour of Jackie's, went aboard her at the age of seven, soon after she was brought to North Shields, and was badly seasick. When fishing this vessel from North Shields Jackie would go out at four o'clock in the morning and return by eight in the evening. He and his crew would then retire to the Low Lights Tavern on Brewhouse Bank, but he would be home by nine o'clock and soon in bed ready for the next early morning start, rising at half past three. During this time he would work ten day spells, starting on a Monday and finishing on a Thursday. In the 1970s his boat broke down and a new engine was fitted, along with other work, at The Haddock Shop dry dock, off Clive Street at North Shields. She had a further refit in the 1980s. In recent years *Karen Obbekaer* may be found at the north bank of the Tyne, at Lemington Point, along the west end of Scotswood. Here she lies rotting, a sad shadow of her former self.

Jackie allowed the author to copy a sequence of three photographs of the *Karen Obbekaer*, taken in 1980 by an unknown photographer aboard *Girl Irene*, whose skipper was Tommy Scorer. The two fishing vessels were pair-trawling at the time. Along the bottom rope at the net mouth were rubber discs, twelve to fourteen inches in diameter, which bounced over the sea bed, but did not rotate. The rubber discs were used instead of the large and heavy metal balls sometimes employed by other

HAULING THE CATCH
Karen Obbekaer (BCK 134) pair trawling from Shields. The catch is partially aboard, 1980. Photograph courtesy of Jackie Weatherstone. Third photograph in a sequence of 3 – see text for explanation. Photographer unknown

vessels, but which would have made the net too heavy for Jackie's boat to haul. The three photographs were taken in the following order:

- the net starts to be pulled alongside. The 'dog line' stretches out into the water;

- the net, full of fish, floating alongside the vessel;

- part of the haul is now aboard, the rest still floating in the net alongside. Due to the weight of fish aboard, the red line along the lower hull (recorded in pictures 1 and 2) is now below water. Jackie said this was a "fantastic haul" with 60-70 boxes of fish, including some large cod.

The third photograph in the sequence is shown here along with a fourth photograph, also taken in 1980 from *Girl Irene*, of Jackie's boat in the North Sea while fishing from North Shields.

AT SEA
Karen Obbekaer (BCK 134) while pair trawling in the North Sea, 1980. Photograph courtesy of Jackie Weatherstone, taken from *Girl Irene*. Photographer unknown

After his time fishing with *Karen Obbekaer*, she lay at the fish quay for two more years while Jackie owned and fished a coble called *Conquest*. She was over ten metres in length and used during the summer salmon season. She was decommissioned and broken up in the early 1990s. To cover harbour dues the *Karen Obbekaer* was sold by the Port of Tyne to Mickey Devlin. Mr Devlin was a scrap man who had barges based on the south side of the Tyne, often used as platforms for river diving operations. Subsequently Jackie purchased another coble at North Shields, which he called *KJB*, and fished with her for several years. The 'K' stood for Karen, his daughter, the 'J' stood for Jackie and 'B' was for Beryl, his wife. Before Jackie bought her, this coble was originally called *Mer Mariner* then *Anne Fair*. The coble had been built more strongly than normal for such a vessel, for someone who was living abroad at the time. She had been kept at St Peter's, on the Tyne, but was not well used, and some of the planking split causing her to sink after filling with rainwater which caused her wood to split further. A gentleman called Bill Stone bought the coble, raised her from the river bottom, shortened her to less than ten metres and renamed her to *Anne Fair*, after his wife. Jackie sold the coble to Roy Elliott in 2006, and Roy renamed her to *Stacey E* (after his daughter) and continues to fish with her locally.

KJB / STACEY E
Stacey E (SN 332) in the Gut at North Shields fish quay. Owner Roy Elliott hauls up the catch on 20 October 2013. This coble was previously owned by Jackie Weatherstone as KJB

"Cobles are just about finished now," Jackie said. "They are flat-bottomed so two or three men can pull them onto a beach with a tractor," but he went on to say this is no longer such a necessity. In the past men would haul nets and pots onto cobles by hand at the stern and these boats had a device called a 'dummy box' into which the propeller could be lifted and so stop entanglement around the propeller blades

when being hauled. A universal coupling, on the prop shaft of these older cobles, ensures the propeller can be lifted like this above the water line. When Jackie fished with Albert Dick from the Haven at Tynemouth, Jackie would shoot the net from the rear of the coble while Albert rowed with two "bloody great oars" that he used to cross as he rowed. They would then drift with the nets for two or three hours before hauling after lifting the two-bladed propeller into the 'dummy box'. Hauling the nets gave Jackie calluses along the little finger on his left hand. Now cobles have a 'net-gobbler' or automatic hauler for hauling up nets and pots very quickly and these are often positioned forward on the vessel – lessening the risk of entanglement with the propeller and negating the need for a 'dummy box'. Roy Elliott's coble *Stacey E* (previously *KJB*) has a 'dummy box', Jackie explained, and Roy shoots his lines with the engine running so the pots and nets normally shoot themselves.

"In the summer you get 'slump' on the nets as algae stick to them. So we used to hose down the nets, but now when the net is shot from the stern of the coble the wash from the rotating propeller cleans off the 'slump'," Jackie told the author. He also said that North Shields coble (or pot) men are now able to work alone, since the net hauler and roller on their vessel lifts the lobster pots right onto a bench on the boat. "Then it is a one-man operation to clean out the pot and put fresh bait inside ready to re-shoot by throwing out the dahn and steaming ahead. Then the pots automatically shoot from the stern as the line feeds out." Jackie thinks the automatic hauler has made the coble almost redundant. "At one time there were seventy sailing cobles fishing out of Cullercoats," he continued. "Albert Dick had fished on a sailing coble at one time and his brother, Bolan, also fished from one and was drowned off Tynemouth north pier. His body was found on the rocks at low

JACKIE, SECOND PORTRAIT
At his North Shields fish quay store, 5 May 2013

tide." Jackie thought bad weather was the cause of this accident, and said that Albert did not talk about it much. Albert had lived in a cottage above the Black Middens, beside the Tynemouth Life Brigade watch house, and his store hut still stands in the Haven near the yacht club. Local fisherman Don McNeill has used this hut for many years now.

In 1939 Jackie's family was the first to move into Knott's Flats, overlooking the river mouth. Against the 'tow wall' (beneath the promenade below the flats), he said, are still the remains of two marks on the rocky shore where two bombs hit during the Second World War. He said they are arc-shaped markings, faint now, but previously well demarcated and they would fill with water. At the end of Lloyd's hailing station jetty a man used to shout, "Where are you bound?" to passing ships leaving the river; this was for insurance and tracking purposes. Jackie could hear this voice quite clearly from Knott's Flats where he lived. He remembers waking one morning and looking out of the window at the family home and seeing a ship getting washed ashore at South Shields, at the beach inside the Groyne. Low down on the north side, at the Black Middens, there had been a tall post with a pointed top, called a 'Skeleton Post', to warn shipping of the dangerous rocks here. "Well," he said, "the ship had knocked it over this morning as she was washed towards the South Shields

EXERCISING THE DOGS
With Kim and Cassie on the fish quay sands with Knott's Flats behind, 26 May 2013

CHECKING THE 'MONK'
Examining his handiwork at the fish quay, a lobster pot for fisherman Alan Dobson,
9 June 2012

shore. The skeleton post was never replaced." As he watched, a breeches buoy was attached to the ship and manned by 30-40 people on the shore in the storm. He said he would always remember a man and his dog being pulled from the boat by the breeches buoy and dipping into the water two or three times on the way to land. As the man reached the shore he leapt up and ran up the beach. Jackie told me of how, when he was a lad, the fishing boats here used coal, and barges would ply up and down off-loading their black cargo to the vessels tied at the quayside.

His dad used to cross linnets and canaries to get better songsters, when living at Knott's Flats. Jackie mentioned that the owner of Marshalls fish and chip shop (*The Fryery by the Priory*, Front Street, Tynemouth), Michael Ray, had once worked at Lilburn's on the fish quay and would baby sit Jackie's young daughter in the latter part of the 1970s. Lilburn's dealt with salmon, including Jackie's locally caught fish of the time.

Jackie still has a store at the fish quay where he makes lobster pots for the fishermen and hay nets for horses. His daughter has always been involved with horses and Jackie's hay nets have a narrow mesh in order to act as slow feeders. Of lobster pots he said "They used to be made from willow and would last one season … they needed to make new pots every year and the boats would fish only thirty pots a year. Then they started to use plastic, then steel. The way we wrap these steel pots means they will last for ten years. Boats now have 600-800 pots out …" In the winter Jackie works at his store for two or three hours each morning and this pays for the cost of the store. When the winter sun gets out and shines from the south onto his store it is like a sun trap up to midday, but as the sun moves further round, his position at the store cools. He does not watch a lot of television and is happy to be pottering at the quay accompanied by one of his dogs.

While working nowadays, he's often accompanied by his German Shepherd dogs. Up to 2009 - 2010 he owned Tim, quite a rare black-haired example, and Tara. After they died he became the owner of another two German Shepherds … Kim and Cassie. When he got her, Cassie was eight months old and had been continually locked up by her previous owner. She was very dirty when Jackie received her and he had great difficulty cleaning her at first. Kim was a six year old bitch who had been maltreated by her previous owner and, up until Jackie's care, she had been used for breeding. Jackie has had both dogs spayed and they can still be quite wary of strangers following their early experiences. They like to lie quietly behind Jackie as he works at his fish quay store. He normally exercises them each morning in the river mouth below Knott's Flats or near Lord Collingwood's Monument. Jackie's wife, Beryl, ran the Northeast England German Shepherd dog rescue organisation for thirty years, saving dogs from mistreatment and ensuring they went to good homes. His grandson has a pony and comes down to the quay to help and watch his grandfather. Of his association with the sea and fish quay, Jackie stated, "It's not a job, it's a way of life."

WITH THE GIRLS
Jackie relaxes outside his fish quay store with Cassie (sitting) and Kim (lying), 21 April 2012

Kevin Mole

Retired fisherman and lifeboat man, full-time mechanic of Tynemouth lifeboat 1987 - 2014

PORTRAIT
Kevin Mole at the lifeboat station, 1 June 2012. In the background is Tynemouth lifeboat *Spirit of Northumberland*

Kevin's father Dougie Mole (born in 1926) worked on a fishing boat out of Seahouses and later bought a double-ended ex-ship's lifeboat *Aquarius* (in the 1960s), as well as owning one or two other small fishing vessels at different times. Dougie was a volunteer Seahouses lifeboat crewman between 1962 and 1971 starting on the Liverpool class lifeboat *Grace Darling*. From the *Grace Darling* he progressed to become mechanic with the subsequent Seahouses lifeboat *Edward and Mary Lester* which was in service at Seahouses from 1967 - 1989. The *Edward and Mary Lester* was a tractor and trailer lifeboat that was launched from the beach. A memorable lifeboat rescue for Dougie Mole involved the *RNLB Grace Darling*. There was bad weather and the lifeboat was required to shelter at the Kettle, in the Inner Farne

GRACE DARLING
Lifeboat *RNLB Grace Darling* was on station at Seahouses from 1954 to 1967. Photograph by courtesy of RNLI Seahouses

69

Island group, from 17 to 19 November 1962. When their food was exhausted, on 18 November, an RAF Shackleton aircraft was requested to drop food with a line over the boat. That night the lifeboat crew sheltered on Inner Farne Island after a daring helicopter lift from their vessels – the Holy Island lifeboat was also involved in this rescue. The next day the weather moderated and the crew were lifted back to their vessels and able to return safely to North Sunderland Harbour. The crew was drenched by the heavy seas very soon after leaving the harbour on 17th and this together with the cold and length of service made the lifeboat honorary secretary (Mr T.W.A. Swallow) very concerned for his men. Dougie served as Seahouses Harbour Master from 1975 - 1987 and later worked on the *Admiral Collingwood* sail training vessel based with the Wellesley Nautical School at Blyth. Dougie assisted as a skipper of the *Admiral Collingwood* which had berths for about twelve passengers / trainees as well additional berths for the skipper and crew. The vessel would sail up and down the coast visiting such places as the river Tyne, Farne Islands and Berwick.

DOUGIE MOLE
Dougie Mole, lifeboat mechanic, Seahouses, c.1972. © Peter Loud

Kevin went to Seahouses Primary School (now a First School) followed by Seahouses County Secondary School. As his father was a fisherman and lifeboat man at Seahouses, Kevin was always around boats as a youngster at the harbour there. He would play on his father's boat *Aquarius* and other small boats around the harbour which he would hop on and off happily around the ages of ten and eleven. He was however then too young to go out to sea on *Aquarius*. Kevin left school at sixteen and started work with Billy Shiel in Seahouses. Billy at that time was a fisherman as well as running vessels taking visitors out to the Farne Islands bird and seal sanctuary during the summer season. Kevin worked lobster pots with Billy in the morning and later in the day would help crew the vessels visiting the Farnes. The Farne Island trips left Seahouses daily at 10:00 (to Staple Island), 13:00 (to Inner Farne) and 15:30 (for a sail around or out to land at Longstone Island) depending on the weather and tides. This work with Billy Shiel was seasonal during the better weather of the spring, summer and early autumn months whereas in the winter Kevin worked during this period with J.W. Thorburn & Sons at Seahouses. At Thorburn's Kevin was a filleter of all sorts of fish including haddock, codling, whiting and salmon (which were smoked at Seahouses). Kevin would visit the evening fish market at Eyemouth and the morning market at North Shields with David Thorburn during the week … they would travel by wagon to buy fish to return with to Seahouses for processing. The Eyemouth evening fish markets were daily from about four or five o' clock, but when visiting the North Shields early morning market they would arrive about half past six. They would normally visit the North Shields market on a Thursday or Friday morning as that was when there were most fish for sale and therefore prices were lower, whereas they visited Eyemouth harbour market daily.

EDWARD AND MARY LESTER
RNLB Edward and Mary Lester at Seahouses harbour. Dougie Mole is wearing the white-topped hat. This lifeboat was based at Seahouses from 1967 to 1989.
© Peter Loud

During the time Kevin worked with Billy Shiel he would also accompany occasional evening tourist boat trips to Holy Island and they would land there depending on the tide. Kevin remembers normally being slightly inebriated when leaving Holy Island after spending some time in the pubs there including the Crown and Anchor. The National Trust licensed certain boats to land at Inner Farne and Staple Island, but those unlicensed boats would sail around the islands or land at Longstone Island for which a permit was not required.

Then in his late teens or early twenties Kevin started trawling from Seahouses as a crewman on different boats fishing on day trips for prawns, clams, dogfish and whitefish, but he never fished for herring. Kevin also helped crew a vessel *Ocean Maid* taking parties of anglers and divers from Seahouses. *Ocean Maid* was owned by Brian Powton who ran the diving lodge at Seahouses. Brian seems to have been a footballer in the 1950s – and is named under the juniors / reserves for Newcastle United, and later with the clubs of Preston North End, Hartlepool United and North Shields. Kevin said that Brian was a big man with a lovely nature who did not originate from Seahouses, but had moved there. When Brian took ill, Kevin took over as skipper of the vessel for a period.

D-535
Inshore lifeboat D-535 on station at the fish quay, 2 March 2008

D-693
D class inshore lifeboat *Mark Noble* (D-693) in the lifeboat house,
15 February 2011

Then Kevin got a job with FMA (Fishermens Mutual Association) at Eyemouth during which (from his mid to late twenties) he was an agent for the Seahouses trawlers and potting boats. This job lasted a few years until Kevin was aged 28. During all Kevin's time at Seahouses, from an early age, he was involved with the lifeboat and then he heard (in 1987) of a permanent full-time vacancy with the Tynemouth lifeboat for which he applied and was successful. Kevin was a lifeboat crewman at Seahouses from 1975 - 1987 on the *Edward and Mary Lester*, but he was never fortunate enough to serve with his father. However Kevin's son Bobby is part of the crew at Tynemouth and he and Kevin have performed a number of jobs together with the lifeboat.

At North Shields fish quay, Kevin has worked on the lifeboats *George and Olive Turner* (Arun class) and *Spirit of Northumberland* (Severn class) as well as the relief boats and their station inshore lifeboats. Part of Kevin's role was training volunteers in such matters as health and safety, safe operation of machinery and electronics as well as application of machinery (for example what to use and when to use it). Kevin also taught operating parameters for machinery, i.e. where their limits are, for

example different types of ropes and the point at which they will part when bearing certain weights and loads. Kevin would teach his trainees safety of operation and the fact that lifeboats must always be left in a state of readiness. At the fish quay Kevin would normally be on station weekdays during office hours dealing with paper work, routine maintenance, etc, but of course the job is 24 hours 'on call' and he must fit in training when appropriate with the volunteer crew members. Compared to Kevin's early experiences with lifeboats all the modern technology, computers, communications, vhf facilities, etc are new. So Kevin started from scratch with such things. During Kevin's latter time with Tynemouth lifeboat station there were an average of 65 to 70 lifeboat 'jobs' each year, while thirty years ago at Seahouses there would not be as many calls since there were less pleasure boats. Kevin said that the job had not really changed in his experience in that they still get called out to people who need help. The lifeboat crew members may rib their friends about callouts later if they should happen to be on the receiving end of a rescue.

Kevin had a coble called *Challenge* (SH 193), which was built in 1972. She came from Newbiggin where the previous owner was going to burn her since the engine was seized and no longer running. However Kevin said he would like to have the

17-20
Spirit of Northumberland returns to her fish quay berth, 4 October 2009. In the distance the Amsterdam ferry returns to the river Tyne

BOARDING BOAT
Michael Nugent (left) and Kevin Mole aboard the Tynemouth lifeboat boarding boat, 4 October 2009

RNLB OSIER
Relief lifeboat *RNLB Osier* (17-34) on station at the fish quay, 8 June 2008

coble and he towed her by sea to North Shields fish quay in the winter of 2007 - 2008. The coble had been out of the water for three years, had dried out and cracks appeared in her body. However once Kevin got her back in the water, after about 24 hours the wooden structure started to heal and swell so the gaps closed again. Kevin mentioned that owners used to deliberately sink their boats when they were unused – this would allow the wood to avoid drying and cracking ashore. He went on to say that when boat owners store a wooden boat ashore they may put a net over which stops direct sunlight shining on the wood and so making it less prone to drying and twisting or 'crine' (an old Northumberland word meaning to shrink or shrivel up). *Challenge* still had the same engine from her previous owners, but Kevin worked to free it allowing it to run sweetly once again. He was to use *Challenge* purely for pleasure and she was later sold.

THREESOME
In the foreground is Kevin's coble *Challenge* and behind lies *Spirit of Northumberland* as DFDS Seaways ferry *King of Scandinavia* departs, 12 April 2008

Kevin's wife is Debbie and they have a son Bobby and daughter Laura. Their faithful old black Labrador called Blue loved the lifeboat station … he was put to sleep in December 2013 at the age of almost 15 years. They also own Spyder, a Shar-pei bitch, which they regularly walk on the small beach beside the lifeboat station.

Kevin retired in January 2014 after 38-39 years of service with the RNLI including 26 years as full-time mechanic with the Tynemouth lifeboats.

KEVIN AT WORK
Aboard the boarding boat at Tynemouth lifeboat station, North Shields fish quay, 23 August 2009

Michael Nugent

Fisherman and lifeboat man, coxswain of Tynemouth lifeboat 2001 - present

Michael originates from Cullercoats and his earliest maritime experiences stem from here. His dad Geoff fished from Cullercoats and used a rowing boat to get to and from his coble moored just off the harbour, so Michael was immersed in fishing life from about five years of age. His dad fished for lobsters and salmon and Michael would go with him before his school day started and during weekends and school holidays. Cobles his father had in those early days were *Admiral* (SN 3) followed by *Flying Spray* (SH 3). He left Marden High School at the age of sixteen (1985) and continued to experience many different kinds of fishing, firstly during a one year YTS (Youth Training Scheme) placement on the fishing vessel *Christine Nielsen* under skipper Cliff Ellis. During his year with the *Christine Nielsen* he travelled to the German coast (off Heligoland) and up to the Norwegian sector on seven- to twelve-day trips where he was treated as a full crew member. He said that Cliff Ellis was a good skipper, but a hard task master. During this year Michael learnt a lot, but his preference was for inshore fishing which is where his grounding had been with his father.

So at the age of seventeen he fished with his brother David on a coble called *Providence* (SN 9) from Cullercoats and North Shields, and a year later Michael was fishing in *Snowflake* (BF 309; later re-registered as SN 1) owned by his father. Before progressing on to *Snowflake*, Michael had short spells with *Sunbeam* (SN 92), skipper Peter Fairbairn (fisherman Peter Clark's maternal grandfather), from whom

PORTRAIT
Tynemouth Severn class lifeboat *Spirit of Northumberland* lies behind Michael at North Shields fish quay, 28 May 2012

77

Michael also learnt a lot, and *Challenge* (SN 51). Michael skippered the *Snowflake* with an additional two crew members until the early 1990s when she was sold and he progressed onto the coble *Enterprise* (BH 108). His brother David in the meantime had been fishing from *Providence* and had a bad experience when he was washed with the coble onto the rocks under the High Point off Whitley Bay (where the pipe comes onto the rocky shore and many anglers like to fish) and the boat was wrecked. David was "shaken, but not stirred" by this experience and he worked ashore for a while and the wrecked *Providence* was replaced with *Enterprise* which Michael said was a nice boat.

With *Snowflake* Michael had fished from North Shields mainly for prawns and sometimes whitefish. In the winter his fishing trips lasted single days, while during the summer he would visit the Dab Hole, 50 to 70 miles east by south from the Tyne, on three- to five-day trips. Sometimes during the summer he would fish *Snowflake* from Eyemouth. *Snowflake* carried ice for chilling the catch, i.e. it was 'old style' and did not have the latest refrigeration units which the likes of the *Christine Nielsen* possessed for keeping the catch fresh for longer periods. The two brothers then fished with *Enterprise* (from the early 1990s) for a time (until David got a job ashore after

SNOWFLAKE
Snowflake (SN 1) leaving the fish quay, 15 July 1986

which Michael continued alone for a few years), lobster fishing in summer and in the winter catching fish as well as lobsters. They fished her from Cullercoats and had early morning starts at four or five o' clock, with the dawn, returning mid morning, then during the rest of the day making lobster pots and carrying out repairs. In 1997 Michael started to fish *Theodoron* (BH 165), a larger coble, from North Shields and David returned to fish on *Enterprise*. With *Theodoron* Michael fished cod nets in winter and drift-netted for salmon in the summer – he continued with this type of fishing throughout the 1990s on *Enterprise* at first followed by *Theodoron*. Meanwhile *Enterprise* was sold and Michael's dad Geoff bought, and David fished, the wooden boat *Adventure* (SN 351) from North Shields in the mid 1990s.

From 1985, at the age of seventeen, Michael was involved as a volunteer with the lifeboat at Cullercoats until he bought *Theodoron* (in 1997) at which time he moved his fishing to North Shields and switched his allegiance to volunteer with the Tynemouth lifeboat. At Cullercoats he had worked with the D and C class inshore

LOBSTERS
Michael's catch of the day, lobsters at the fish quay on 16 June 2013

FREYA
Freya (BH 121) gets a new coat of paint,
North Shields fish quay, 6 January 2007

VALIANT STAR
Michael works aboard *Valiant Star* (H 73),
North Shields fish quay, 23 February 2008

lifeboats followed by the Atlantic 21 (i.e. 21 feet in length). The current Cullercoats'
lifeboat is an Atlantic 85 (i.e. 8.5 metres in length). He started as a crew member
at Cullercoats lifeboat station and progressed to become helmsman on all three
boats mentioned from this period. From 1997 at the Tynemouth lifeboat station he
worked with the *George and Olive Turner* and the current *Spirit of Northumberland*
all-weather lifeboats as well as the D class inshore station lifeboats.

At Tynemouth lifeboat Michael moved quickly from crew member to deputy coxswain
on the *George and Olive Turner*. Then in November 2001 he started in a permanent
full time role (as 'Coxswain Designate') with the Tynemouth lifeboat progressing to
full coxswain two months later when Martin Kenny retired from the position. He

continued to own *Theodoron* for a further two years alongside working for the RNLI at which point *Theodoron* and wooden *Adventure* (SN 351) were sold and fibreglass *Adventure* (BH 2) was bought by Geoff, Michael and his brother David. In November 2009 his old *Theodoron* was fishing out of Bridlington while in the winter of 2013/14 fibreglass *Adventure* (BH 2) is still based at North Shields. Wooden *Adventure* (SN 351) went down to Wales after she was sold by Geoff and was later owned and fishing off the Scottish Western Isles, but re-named to *Trust* and was for sale again in late 2009. Since 2007 Michael has owned and worked with a further three inshore cobles while lobster fishing close to the lifeboat station so that he can respond to callouts in good time. These cobles are: *Freya* (BH 121; fished 2007 to early 2008), *Valiant Star* (H 73; fished early 2008 to late 2009) and *Claire Louise* (MH 296; purchased in 2009). The latter vessel was renovated (by Michael and Kevin Mole)

THEODORON
Preparing to bait his pots aboard *Theodoron* (AH 165) at the fish quay. In the background are Tynemouth lifeboat *Spirit of Northumberland* (17-20) and coble *Challenge*. 5 February 2012

VALIANT STAR
Taking *Valiant Star* out to check his lobster pots – passing the Groyne, (South Shields), 13 April 2008

with the creation of a wheelhouse and new deck before Michael started using her with lobster pots – then renamed to *Theodoron* (AH 165) in April 2010. *Theodoron* was re-registered as BH 165 in August 2012.

Michael states that lifeboating has changed during his involvement, becoming more automated and computerised with more strict health and safety regulations and introduction of litigation legislation (for example in case of damage caused by a lifeboat to the vessel they may be rescuing, although he said that this situation had never arisen at the Tynemouth station). Michael goes on to say that the RNLI has adapted to modern times and must be careful to protect its reputation and crew as well as provide and care for facilities and craft. He said, "The lifeboat job and how you do it has not really changed. However the majority of the crew used to be seafaring folk while more training is required nowadays as crew come from a wide variety of often non-seafaring backgrounds." Michael is also the Station Training Coordinator for Tynemouth lifeboat. Initial courses for crew on the big all-weather lifeboats include sea safety and fire-fighting. Younger crew may start on the D class inshore boat and would have introductory training, learn about navigation and how boats are built, etc. The upper age limit for the D class vessels is 45 and for the offshore vessels 55 with a possible five year extension depending on fitness and passing annual medical examinations. Michael has carried out all the different lifeboat roles, which is required grounding as a coxswain, and has always enjoyed his experience with the lifeboats which his dad was involved with before him.

Particular experiences etched on Michael's memory with the Tynemouth lifeboat are when the yacht *Signature* rolled at the bar at the mouth of the Tyne on 3 April 1998 ("a hairy event") and when the *Jann Denise II* (SH 273) was lost on 17 November 2004. Some details follow.

The yacht *Signature* 'had been knocked down by a heavy sea entering the River Tyne and lost several crew members overboard' according to the letters of thanks to coxswain Martin Kenny and crew members Edwin Chapple, Geoffrey Cowan, Kevin Mole and Michael Nugent. A high easterly swell 'of approximately 35 feet' was running and 'breaking over the full length and width of the piers' with easterly force

SNOW SCENE
Coxswain Michael Nugent at the stern of *Spirit of Northumberland* awaiting the rest of the crew, 1 January 2010. They are going to assist a surfer off Trow Rocks, South Shields

3 winds as *RNLB George and Olive Turner* slipped her moorings at 13:13. By 13:27 two bodies had been recovered from the sea and a third casualty with severe head wound, swimming weakly, was also recovered. The RAF helicopter attended and assisted, taking the conscious man from the lifeboat at 13:33 and returning so its paramedic-trained winch man could help when the lifeboat arrived at the Port of Tyne pontoon. Resuscitation attempts were maintained throughout on the two unconscious men by the lifeboat crew who also looked after the remaining yacht crew members before their transportation to hospital.

The *Jann Denise II* (9.79 metres in length) foundered and sank on 17 November 2004 with the loss of her crew, Robert Temple (skipper and owner) ... and his brother Brian, both of whom were experienced fishermen. The vessel was last sighted by *Frem*, another local fishing vessel, at approximately 12:30 when she was 'steaming back to the port of North Shields after early completion of a fishing trip due to worsening weather conditions' (Marine Accident Investigation Branch, Report No 15/2005, August 2005). The vessel foundered 5.5 miles south-south-east of the River Tyne. The vessel was later salvaged and the MAIB report records she '... began to take water in her aft steering compartment and her engine room due to the poor structural condition of the vessel.' The report continues, the vessel was 'swamped by seas' and '... she sank rapidly by the stern. There was no time to transmit a "Mayday".' 'At the time of the accident the weather conditions had deteriorated to a westerly force 6 to 7, creating a very confused swell.' The alarm was raised at the harbour at 16:00 when the skipper of another vessel realised *Jann Denise II* was not in the harbour and she could not be contacted by VHF radio. Coxswain Michael Nugent was informed and he, in turn, informed the Humber Coastguard and a search was commenced involving the rescue helicopter, three lifeboat stations, the Sunderland Coastguard Rescue Team, Tynemouth Volunteer Life Brigade plus at least 15 local fishing vessels. That evening the search was called off at 21:30 after what was believed to be the wreck was discovered by a new echo sounder "mark" on the seabed (later confirmed by a diver's survey on 21 November). The search was resumed on 18 November and debris was retrieved. The search was called off as light faded and 1200 square miles had been checked. On 12 December 2004 the vessel was recovered from the seabed. Tests confirmed concerns over the stability of the vessel, but up to this time there was no requirement for vessels under 12 m to comply with any kind of stability criteria. Due to the worsening weather the vessel's catch (weighing approx. 400 kgs) had been left in the cod end of her net aboard the vessel as she steamed for port. The vessel was inspected by the Maritime and Coastguard Agency in 2001, but this excluded an examination of her structural condition since there was no requirement to do so. The MAIB report goes onto state that ' … had *Jann Denise II* been subject to the same survey regime as that of larger vessels, this accident might have been avoided.' The vessel carried a life raft though it failed to operate correctly. Subsequent to the accident actions were taken in relation to vessels under 15 metres, including (a) a review of the Instructions for Safety Inspections, and (b) a review of the Code of Practice for the safety of small fishing vessels of less than 15m length.

Using his experience Michael plays to the strengths of his crew and tries to find roles to which they are all individually suited, catering to their natural abilities. "All crew should be able to perform the deck jobs", Michael goes on to say, "… and someone with, for example, a computer background, may be filtered to working with the navigational instruments." "The crew all work as a team", Michael continues, "… and they generally integrate and naturally form a crew, but they each need to be able to perform many roles."

MEDALS
Michael's RNLI medals
Left: The Queen's Golden Jubilee medal (Awarded 2002)
Right: The Queen's Diamond Jubilee medal (Awarded 2012)

Since becoming coxswain at Tynemouth Michael has carried out a few spells as relief coxswain, generally of about one week at a time, at Spurn Head as well as Islay and Weymouth. He continues in his combined roles as coxswain for the Tynemouth lifeboat and local inshore fisherman. He is married to Emma and they have a young daughter Lily and two faithful short-haired border terriers called Rosie and Scampi, who also love the lifeboat station. Michael's tall son Christopher is also a North Shields fisherman, at times working with his grandfather Geoff aboard *Adventure* (BH 2).

THEODORON
Michael guides *Theodoron* (BH 165) into the fish quay Gut to land his catch, 31 March 2013

THREESOME
At the fish quay with Michael's haul of crabs and lobsters. From left: John Rogers (local fisherman), Geoff Nugent and Michael Nugent, 9 June 2013

Michael Smith

One-time marine division policeman, current North Shields fisherman and artist

Born in Newcastle-upon-Tyne (in 1946), brought up from a young baby in Alnwick and apprenticed at the age of sixteen to the Electricity Board, Michael got the fishing bug early. While an apprentice he would travel by bus, on his days off, to Amble to go out fishing, "I would go out on any boat I could!" he recounted. The first boat he ventured out with was called *Ocean Vanguard*, owned and skippered by Tom Handyside. She was a 37-39 foot seine-net boat with small gunnels, rising to about a foot above the deck, so that the net could be handled aboard. Due to lack of DTI (Dept of Trade and Industry) inspections in those days, there were no such things as shelter decks to give the crew some protection. Nowadays inspections are carried out on fishing vessels every two to three years to ensure health and safety, seaworthiness, etc. (see references to Maritime and Coastguard Agency). This boat had a crew of six, ("four of them were Handysides. There was skipper Tom Handyside, well seventyish and still going to sea, his son Tom Handyside and his son also called Tom.") There was also an Eddie Handyside, uncle to the young grandson Tom. Eddie was a master builder, in his forties at this time, but one of the crew had left and so Eddie was needed to help crew the vessel. So aboard *Ocean Vanguard* they would steam for about one hour off Amble to fish … first shooting the dahn buoy and six or seven coils of leaded rope, ("A coil may be about a hundred fathoms … not sure," recounted Michael). Then the wing of the net would follow over the side of the boat, followed by the belly and cod end and another coil, then the boat would turn to run

PORTRAIT
26 August 2006, in the background *Sophie Louise II* (SSS 678) is berthed at the fish quay beneath the Old High Light

87

back to the dahn buoy to bring it over the winch. The seine net would sit at the bottom of the sea rising perhaps twenty feet, and the ropes would be pulled taught so the net sat up from the sea floor. As soon as the dahn buoy was started to be winched the net would be hauled. "It would take one and a quarter hours to shoot and haul," Michael told me. Of the crew of six the skipper spent most of his time in the wheelhouse. "It was nearly always poor weather when I went out with him," he remembered. The Handysides would be happy working on deck with such low gunnels, "but I was nearly on my hands and knees ... not used to it," Michael remarked. From Amble the boats fished Mondays to Fridays only, so he would take a day off work to go and fish. "The Shields folk were called heathens, by the Amble folk, as they went to sea on Saturdays and Sundays!" he informed me. Michael would get the bus and stay overnight at Tom Handyside's home, getting up at three in the morning to go off fishing. At this time Michael was sixteen to seventeen years old.

("Eddie Handyside was drowned at the Amble pier ends ... I was not there that day. The funeral at the church was packed – he was a popular lad.") Apparently the weather had been poor, but old Tom had taken out *Ocean Vanguard* and turned back as they could not fish in the conditions. At the bar, where the sea and fresh water meet at the pier ends, there was a confused sea and the skipper positioned all his crew behind the wheel house. But the sea came from both sides and washed Eddie towards the south pier; he was heard to call out twice. Michael continued, "Young Tommy was going to go to get him, but they stopped him." Eddie was just in his forties and had told Michael he was starting to enjoy the fishing. Michael may have taken Eddie's place in the crew, but was still an apprentice with the Electricity Board and said, "My mam and dad would not let me at the time."

APAPA
Michael was with *Apapa* for around three months. Photograph by kind permission of Ian Coombe, site manager (mnnostalgia.com), Merchant Navy Nostalgia

On finishing his apprenticeship Michael left the Electricity Board and joined the merchant navy as an electrical fitter, although he had intended going to Hull or Grimsby to fish, but was courting at the time and his girlfriend did not want him to go fishing. So he was employed with the 'Blue Funnel Line' on a few different boats and eventually went deep sea on the *Apapa*, a mail ship which went down the west coast of Africa as far as Lagos. He was with *Apapa* for around three months, but was lonely for his wife … they had married during this time. So he left the merchant navy returning to Newcastle to join the Newcastle City Police Force in the late 1960s

LUC ARRIVES
Michael prepares to throw rope and berth *Luc* at the fish quay, 4 December 2013. In the background is the Tynemouth all-weather lifeboat

aged 22 years. The last two of his ten years with the police were spent with the marine division patrolling the Tyne. They worked a three shift system for 24 hours a day and seven days a week. Each police boat would have a sergeant and two police constables and they patrolled the Tyne looking for signs of criminal activity. For example, merchant navy ships were checked for immigrants and to ensure any ship's dog was locked safely inside a cabin so could not get ashore. The Port of Tyne would inform the police if there were any dogs on board ships, so they could then check daily afterwards to ensure strict regulations were met. Police launches were useful in case of such matters as a person jumping from one of the Tyne bridges, or to investigate any sad report of a body in the river – such as one case attended by Michael. The police force used to take angling trips to Eyemouth and this prompted Michael to ask the skipper of an Eyemouth fishing boat to take him 'off' (i.e. fishing offshore) one time … "and so I got the bug again!" he told me. So he would take days off, fitting in with his police shifts, and at first fished one day a month from Eyemouth. This later led to two days a month, to one day a week and finally to fishing on every day off he had. At Eyemouth the fishing was, like at Amble, only on weekdays, and during this period he fished on the vessel *Guiding Star*, an ex seine net boat that was later rigged for prawns. "Prawn fishing really started at that time, about forty years ago", he confirmed, and Michael also used to go 'off' on boats from Shields "for nowt!" – he just loved the experience. He had one trip aboard *Lindisfarne* (BCK 147) from North Shields, skippered by Cliff Ellis, ("He was the top skipper!"). The trip was two days fishing for sprats …. they caught 80 tons that time. About a year earlier he had been set to sail with Cliff, but the vessel left a day early and Michael missed the trip, so asked another skipper if he could go with their vessel instead … since he had taken time off work, and the skipper agreed. He therefore started fishing one trip a year aboard *Lothian Rose* ("A beautiful boat … the best sea boat I have ever been in.") In *Lothian Rose* Michael fished in the Ekofisk oil field – from thirty miles distance they navigated towards a large gas burner in the field. Michael mentioned that fishing there could produce 200-300 boxes of fish in a day and they were joined by boats from Denmark, Norway and Sweden "all dipping in". Also from North Shields Michael had a couple of trips, for which he received payment, aboard *Janisca*. She was a Scottish vessel (possibly from Anstruther) – the first trip he had was Monday to Thursday, when they – "worked the Dogger Bank, seine netting". He spent the Friday to Sunday with the police force on 6 a.m. to 2 p.m. shifts, and followed this with his second trip, over the next few days, on *Janisca* to the Dogger Bank again. For his two day trip aboard *Lindisfarne*, skipper Cliff Ellis made sure Michael was paid – "about fifty pounds … at least two weeks wages at the time!" recounted Michael.

SALMON FISHING
Coble *Silver Coquet* off the Tyne in search of salmon and sea trout. A painting by Michael Smith

MORNING DEPARTURE
Silver Coquet departs the river Tyne in the early morning of 20 August 2012, at 5:40 a.m. She's towing smaller coble *Marilyn Clark III*

The trip had been a short distance out from St Mary's Island. He continued, "Cliff determined that fish were congregating where sand covered oil pipelines out at sea, where the warmer water attracted feed for the fish." Often Michael was going to sea for no payment, just for the experience.

("There was a big herring fishery off the Farnes and the Scots boats pair-trawled there from North Shields"). These Scottish fishing boats would steam up river to Newcastle at the weekend to tie up there and go to the city pubs. Michael asked the skipper of one of these vessels at Newcastle Quayside, *Atlantic Star*, if he could go with them. A couple of days later, on a Wednesday, they sailed in the afternoon with Michael and towed through the night. They steamed for three hours from port each way and fished for about two hours i.e. the two Scottish boats trawling together (in such 'pair trawling' two trawlers tow one net between them). On this trip, *Atlantic Star* towed for about 12 to 14 minutes and they landed 810 boxes of herring. ("It is the most exciting fishing I have ever been at … there must have been fifty to sixty boats at the same place fishing." "Herring is silver on the slab, but not when they come in from the net – I call it 'shot' … like the lining of a ladies coat … blue, pink, all different colours … herring is just like that!"). Michael continued, "I must have had some nerve in those days … I just asked the skipper – it seemed like a wonderful life, I thought, let's have some of that. I went from one rat race to a worse rat race!" Michael also had some time fishing on day trips for sprats from Shields aboard *Adastra* and *Sunbeam* (SN 92), owned and skippered by Peter Fairbairn.

SEASON'S END
Michael aboard *Silver Coquet* (SN 8) in the Gut, preparing to have her lifted from the water at the end of the salmon season, 31 August 2013

SEASON'S PROGRESS
Michael with Dennis Clark aboard *Silver Coquet* (LH 576) preparing salmon nets, mid-morning on 24 July 2011

OFF-SEASON
Silver Coquet at Cullercoats boatyard,
9 May 2010

END OF SEASON
Silver Coquet (SN 8) being lifted from
the river Tyne at the end of the salmon
season. Michael sits at the stern,
balancing her, 31 August 2013

He 'wrapped in' the police force and bought a Cullercoats coble, *Sweet Remembrance*, using pots, fishing for salmon during the season and using cod nets in winter from North Shields. The coble was sold to his partner at the time and later sold on to someone up the river. After a brief spell as a fish quay security man, while with the North Shields Fishermen's Association, he joined Dennis Clark, helping Dennis's father Doug with jobs on trawler *Luc* (SN 36) while she was being built and completed. *Luc* was built up the river Tyne and Michael helped with all sorts of jobs. Most of the fitting out of *Luc* was done by Doug, Dennis and Michael. When she was ready for fishing, in 1982, Doug was skipper with Dennis as mate and Michael as 'boy'. Later Dennis became skipper and now Dennis's son Peter is skipper, with Michael helping aboard all this time – for the past thirty years or more. At one time *Luc* used to berth at the 'Water Quay' where the lifeboat station now stands, but she now berths just inside the Gut at the 'Knuckle end'. ("I used to say I was the oldest apprentice and youngest granddad on the quay, but now I am still the oldest apprentice, but the youngest great granddad!") One time the 'Lumpers' on the quay (these are the people who lay out the fish on the market) lined up on the 'Water quay' and sang "Grandad" to Michael – this was the song made famous by English actor Clive Dunn, who had a number one hit single with it in January 1971. *"Lumper* is perhaps a term from Hull and Grimsby, they are also called *buskers* here," Michael informed me. With *Luc* the crew used to fish for prawns from the end of August up to March and then use the coble *Silver Coquet* for redfish. Now the coble is fished by Michael and Dennis Clark between the first of June and the end of August for salmon and sea trout.

FISH QUAY ARRIVAL
Trawler *Luc* returns to the fish quay with her catch, 16 February 2008

LUC (SN 36)
Fishing vessel *Luc*, berthed at North Shields fish quay, 20 June 2010

Returning to other topics ... namely Michael's passion for art ... as a lad he went to Alnwick secondary modern school and stayed on after completion of the Northern Counties Leaving Certificate in his fourth year. During his fifth year he was able to pick subjects for GCE studies and selected Art as one, since he always liked this and had been "quite good" at the subject. However the year did not progress well and he

wished for more encouragement from the staff. Not returning to art for many years he then began to borrow library books, and started drawing pictures from sailing books as well as learning about the vessels' rigging. While working for the police force Michael started to attend a day release course at an art college on Bath Lane, Newcastle, near the Gallowgate bus station. However he gave up the course half way through when promoted to the police detective department. "I would like to have gone to art school," Michael said, "but had failed the GCE at school".

When fishing aboard *Luc*, he loved the job and gave up painting due to the hours – which could start at three in the morning and not finish until ten o'clock at night. "Little by little … I took it up again," he remarked. After his interest took hold again he used PVA (poly vinyl acetate / adhesive, a water-based glue and pigment) paints at first, but has progressed to liquid acrylics. He draws many pictures from photographs and

LOVELY NELLY RESCUE
One of Michael's paintings records this rescue off Whitley Bay on New Year's Day 1861

FISH QUAY PANORAMA
Michael's painting shows a great vista from the New High Light, through the Gut and out into the expanse of the Tyne river mouth

is keen on historical subjects related to sailing ships, especially local history with a bent towards fishing. ("With those hours on *Luc* there was no chance to paint during the daylight"). People come to Michael with commissions, for example to paint boats in working situations. He also paints scenes, sometimes for Christmas cards, for local lifeboat stations including: Seahouses, Amble, Newbiggin, Blyth, Cullercoats and Tynemouth. Some of these paintings are raffled with proceeds going to station funds. In early 2012 Michael was working on a new painting, for Cullercoats lifeboat station, of the rescue from the brig *Lovely Nelly* off Whitley Sands on 1st January 1861 during which the cabin-boy (Thomas Thompson) was lost. Michael exhibits his work on lifeboat days and at the RNMDSF (Royal National Mission to Deep Sea Fishermen), North Shields fish quay.

Michael painted a picture that hangs in the office of Jeremy Pritchard (NSFQ Co Ltd Manager from 1993 - 2014). This is a panorama of the fish quay and its fishing boats looking from within the Gut and around to the Groyne at South Shields. "If it had not been for Jeremy the fish quay would be finished. Things were very basic when he came and he got grants for all his important fish quay projects. He has made his mark!" … Michael is a fan! Before tackling the final painting for Jeremy, he worked on a practice painting of the scene and consequently made a few adjustments in the final version. Michael enjoys painting so much he states, "When I retire from fishing hopefully painting will be my living!"

BEN LORA
"Running afore the storm" – from a watercolour by Michael Smith. Trawler *Ben Lora* returns to Shields with Tynemouth castle and priory in the background

Rob Dearman

Worked for HM Customs & Excise on the Northeast England coast, based almost entirely in North Shields, from 1960 - 1963

Rob lived in Gosforth as a youth, left school and went to sea at the age of 16 – joining the Merchant Navy as a deck apprentice and serving for a period of eighteen months. During this period at sea Rob spent time aboard three ships, mostly with Royal Fleet Auxiliary (RFA) *Tidereach* (A96) coming in and out of the River Tyne. RFA *Tidereach* was built at the Wallsend Yard of Swan Hunter & Wigham Richardson (Yard No. 1847) and launched in 1954. This was a tanker that supplied royal naval vessels at sea, for example aircraft carriers would be supplied with fuel oil, diesel and aviation spirit for helicopters, etc, therefore supplying a full range of fuels. On these ships he visited such places as the Baltic ports, Tangier, Mediterranean ports, Narvik and the Lofoten Islands in Northern Norway. At this time the Royal Navy was a massive organisation with a home fleet based in British and European waters covering from the Arctic Circle to Gibraltar. There was also a Mediterranean fleet based at Malta and Gibraltar. Those were the days when Britain was a world power and an example of an exercise in the Northern Cape would involve two aircraft carriers, destroyers and frigates – all of which required fuel. Rob explains, "It was impressive when this fleet, with their RFA tanker, would call in at a port, in Copenhagen for example, and were all berthed at the quayside together. The Royal Marine bands would parade at sunset wearing their white helmets, beating the retreat." *Tidereach* was an RFA

PORTRAIT
Behind stands the tall blue disused ice plant and Scottish trawler *Gratitude* (BF 103) at the west quay, 14 August 2014

99

ship, but part of the Merchant Navy, and therefore the crew were not required to wear naval uniforms. Merchant ships carry no arms and can therefore visit neutral countries for fuel, mail and supplies in times of military action. In the United States Navy all supply ships are part of the US Navy and are therefore armed military ships, thus not allowed to call at neutral ports in those situations. Deciding he did not wish to spend the next forty years at sea Rob left the Merchant Navy and, because this was the time of National Service, spent the next two years in the army after being called up. If he'd spent National Service in the Royal Navy, he would have been required to serve a minimum of nine years as a regular.

TIDEREACH
RFA *Tidereach*, leaving the Tyne and passing North Shields fish quay, date unknown. The Shields Gazette retains copyright

Following National Service Rob joined HM Customs & Excise in 1960, but maintained his interest in shipping. He applied for the role through a Civil Service national recruitment programme and therefore took part in their open competition which involved grammar school type leaving examinations and an interview – Rob's was in Leeds. This was for the uniformed side of HM Customs & Excise called 'The Waterguard', and his induction included a two month training course in London. He had enrolled at the local office in North Shields, but after the two month London course could have been posted anywhere. Fortunately he came back to North Shields to work, while some of his fellow course members found themselves in Goole, at Heathrow airport and on the land boundary in Northern Ireland. Starting as an assistant preventive officer he joined the office at North Shields. This was the last building on the right (Number 67) as you come down Borough Road bank towards the ferry landing. There were about forty staff based there and Rob normally visited the first floor where the Chief Preventive Officer had an office in the corner of the building. However, virtually all of Rob's time on a boarding shift was spent aboard their launch which would tie up at the North Shields ferry landing. This account deals with some of Rob's experience during the period 1960 - 1963 when he was based on the River Tyne at North Shields.

OLD CUSTOM HOUSE
At the bottom of Borough Road, North Shields, 27 April 2012

From their North Shields base, Rob and his colleagues would patrol the lower section of the Tyne providing 24 hour coverage. He made up part of a shift of five staff consisting of two customs officers, a deck hand, the skipper of the launch and an engineer. The boarding customs officers would be a preventive officer and an assistant preventive officer. They would board ships that had come from abroad and clear them for health and to ensure duty free goods were secure. The crew of each ship would complete an overall ship's declaration form which listed each crew member and any personal goods each had which were liable to duty. The ship's captain was responsible for the declaration document and for ensuring all crew members completed it. The chief steward or captain would have a secure locker for duty-free stores. This was locked up while the ship was in port and would hold, for example, several thousand cigarettes and several cases of spirits for a normal decent sized cargo ship.

At that time the river was very busy and their crews would board several ships on each tide. The ships were either boarded when they had berthed or, if they were waiting for a berth, at the permanently positioned river buoys where they waited. These permanently positioned buoys were near Albert Edward Dock and Tyne Commission Quay where the ship sheltered at a position deemed appropriate by the Port of Tyne Authority. Bulk iron ore carriers would discharge at Tyne Dock, from where the cargo was transported to Consett steel works by rail. On modern iron ore carriers the ore is removed with grabs after which a JCB and bulldozer are lowered into the hold to

CUSTOM HOUSE NAMEPLATE
Borough Road, North Shields

complete the job. The hold compartments are nowadays rectangular or square and have no need for large manpower in their discharge. However in the early 1960's ore carriers were often general cargo boats and the ore would get trapped between girders, etc, in the bottom of the ship. This required teams of dockers to go into the hold and shovel the ore into a bucket to be lifted by crane – a labour intensive activity that also meant it took quite some time to discharge such a ship.

MS BRAEMAR
Photograph courtesy of Fred. Olsen

BETWEEN NORTH SEA CROSSINGS
MS Braemar at Tyne Commission Quay, North Shields,
1967. © Chris Morgan

The North Shields Customs and Excise officers also checked the river's regular shipping which included the passenger ferries from Norway and Denmark berthing at Tyne Commission Quay. These ships consisted, in the period 1960 - 1965, of the Braemar I and Blenheim II, of the Fred. Olsen Line, and the TS Leda of the Bergen Line, complemented from 1966 by the Venus and Jupiter. [Braemar I was introduced to the Fred. Olsen fleet in 1953, and joined her sister ship Blenheim II; she maintained the Oslo-Kristiansand-Newcastle service until she was withdrawn in 1975 and sold to become The Philippine Tourist, a casino ship. Blenheim II started her maiden crossing from Oslo to Newcastle on 30th March 1951. She was damaged by fire in 1968, and sold that same year to A/S Uglands Rederi, Grimstad and converted into car-carrier Cilaos. Turbine Ship Leda was built by Swan Hunter on the Tyne and completed in April 1953]. These passenger ferries normally arrived around six a.m., after an overnight passage, and discharged their passengers first thing in the morning. Some of their office staff checked the passengers at the start of their

BLENHEIM II
Arriving in the Tyne on 26 June 1976.
Photograph courtesy of Tyne and Wear
Archives (Reference DF.RIP/18/6/8)

TS LEDA
Bergen Line *TS Leda* at Tyne Commission
Quay, North Shields, in the 1950s.
© Colin Alexander

shift and then they would carry out other duties. When these passenger ferries came into the river their bonded stores were secured in port. These ships also contained retail shops aboard where the goods sold to passengers were subjected to Purchase Tax, the forerunner to VAT.

The Borough Road office regular boarding crews covered the river up as far as Willington Quay, where there was a separate office also with three shifts of five man crews and a launch, similar to North Shields. At Newcastle quayside there were additional customs officers and here a launch had been used up until the late 1950's – especially for checking ships at the then very busy Dunstan coal staithes. DFDS Seaways (a Danish shipping company) ships used to run up to the Newcastle quayside in the 1960's to discharge cargo such as butter, Danish bacon and Carlsberg beer.

The HM Customs & Excise staff would keep up to date with shipping movements by reading the daily Lloyd's List, speaking with Port of Tyne authorities as well as the river pilots and making phone calls, when first on shift for the day, to determine such shipping information. Their main job was to secure the ships stores, check on crew health and allow rummage crews (or 'Black Gangs') to check the ships for contraband goods. The North Shields based customs officers of the Black Gangs (a largely Merchant Navy term) used to cover such harbours and ports as Hartlepool, Seaham, Sunderland, the river Tyne as far as Dunston, Blyth, Amble and up the coast as far as Berwick. The locations outside the Tyne were more normally covered by the 'mobile' crew, which differed from the normal station rummage crews on the river Tyne. A ship's crew declaration document covered their personal supplies, the rest of the ship's duty-free goods were stored in the secure stores … so the Black Gang's job was to search ships for any other duty-free goods that had not been declared. The specially selected 'mobile' crew were paid more than the regular customs boarding or station rummage crews and were composed of more experienced officers receiving a fixed daily payment including two hours of overtime. There were three Black Gangs based at North Shields in the early 1960's i.e. two 'station' crews and the 'mobile', each of four men (normally comprising three assistant preventive officers and one preventive officer), working eight hour shifts. Rob worked in each of these Black Gangs (or rummage crews) for a time … they worked flexibly, also used cars, and could select where to go … adjusting their timings to suit particular shipping movements. The reason for the name Black Gang was partly because the officers

could get dirty (and black) in their searches for contraband – as they rummaged in dirty and oily parts of the ship. There were still a few coal burning ships about at the time and ships' crews sometimes hid contraband under coal in the bunker – so the rummage crew were required to move the coal to search. Goods could also be hidden under plates in engine rooms and ballast tanks – other dirty places! Those ships that had a quick turn around in

DUNSTON STAITHES 1
Dated 1925. Photograph courtesy of Gateshead Libraries (Ref GL003014)

port would not hide contraband in such places since more time was needed to access them and often plates, etc, had to be removed first. However if, for example, a Finnish boat was berthed at Dunston for a week the crew would have time to access such hidey holes. Normally the whole ship's crew would work together to smuggle goods, while crews of various nationalities were observed to differ in the way they smuggled.

The Staithes, Dunston-on-Tyne.

The 'mobile' rummage crew was normally a more experienced crew than each of the two 'station' crews, and was selected from volunteers for a twelve month calendar period. Rob was in the 1963 'mobile' crew. The 'mobile' rummage crew preventive officer would be selected by the port chief preventive officer, and he in turn would usually select his own three assistant preventive officers. The volunteers selected were usually the more experienced, enthusiastic and motivated. 'Mobile' crews were also flexible in the times they could work and had priority in selection of ships they wished to search and ports visited. By contrast the two 'station' crews were appointed on a rota every three months and they worked standard eight hour days, so between the two 'station' crews the daylight high tides were covered (i.e. shifts would start at 06:00, 08:00, 10:00 or 14:00). It was not unheard of for two or more rummage crews to work on one ship, but in North Shields this was the exception other than for ships with a very large crew (i.e. the whale factory ships returning from a season in the Antarctic, for example the *Balaena* (crew capacity of 444, Hector Whaling Company Ltd, London) and *Southern Harvester*. The two aforementioned whaling

DUNSTON STAITHES 2
Date unknown. Photograph courtesy of Gateshead Libraries (Ref GL002333)

ships tended to return annually to Brigham and Cowans yard in South Shields, "Their arrival was announced by the very pungent smell!" The rummage crews adjoining those in North Shields were based in Leith to the north and Middlesbrough to the south … the latter location held two 'station' rummage crews.

Normally ships went to sea on two year articles i.e. the whole crew signed up to the ship for a period of two years. While the ship was abroad the crew were stuck with her during that two year period, but back in a British port within the two year period – a crew member may discharge themselves from the ship if they so wished. Such a tramp steamer may leave for the Far East, but not know exactly when they may return, possibly getting diverted during their voyage. During the Korean War (1950 - 1953) ships' crews were required to sign five year articles. So when articled

W.F. BALAENA
Whale Factory Ship *Balaena*, entering Dry Dock at Hebburn. Photograph courtesy of Tyne and Wear Archives (Reference DX1529/4/7)

ships left port they would want to take quite a lot of duty-free goods – perhaps to last for a two year journey. Such goods may include 400 cases of beer, 20 cases of spirits (and even 20 cases of whisky), plus enough duty-free cigarettes for a two year period. Such duty-free stores onboard ship were secured and under the control of the captain or chief steward, depending on size of the ship, so the crew could not access them while in British ports.

SOUTHERN HARVESTER
Whale factory ship *Southern Harvester* arriving in the Tyne on 28 May 1961. Photograph courtesy of Tyne and Wear Archives (Reference DFRIP/18/52/2)

Deep sea trawlers could get duty free allowances, therefore sometimes their vessel stores would be checked, but this only applied to vessels fishing in areas north and east of certain latitudes and longitudes (such allowances were not granted to boats fishing in more local waters). A common tipple was Johnny Walker Black Label – for example a deep sea trawler may take one case of this on a long trip to Icelandic waters. Normal rummage crews did not consider our own fishing fleet to be a high risk since they were genuine fishermen who were not into getting contraband from other ships offshore. The customs staff were interested in control of revenue and a big revenue risk appeared when foreign fishing fleets appeared – in the 1960's there were Polish, East German and Russian trawlers fishing off the east coast and all around the British coast – which regularly came to North Shields fish quay. The crews were very poorly paid, for example a Polish crew man may receive £9 per month, so these people seemed to be just as interested in smuggling as they were in fishing.

FISH QUAY FROM *TS LEDA*
North Shields fish quay, signal stations, pilot jetty and lifeboat station, 1964. Taken from *TS Leda*. © Chris Morgan

Polish fishing boats, which were of modest sizes, were largely to blame when it came to fishermen smugglers. They probably passed through the Kiel Canal to come to our waters and stocked up en route with cigarettes and Polish spirits to smuggle to the UK for sale. They also bought goods in the UK to smuggle abroad, for example coffee to Germany and clothing to Poland. The skippers were expected to be fishing, but if there was a storm brewing ("or even the slightest bit of a wind, we thought," says Rob), the whole Polish fleet of trawlers would come to the northeast ports of Blyth, North Shields, Sunderland and Seaham for some smuggling. As many as fifty Polish trawlers could come into North Shields fish quay at such a time. The fish quay would quickly fill, so some of the fishing boats would need to moor at Albert Edward Dock and staithes at South Shields. This number of vessels together was impossible for the customs crews to check completely and they would try to intercept some of the smuggling from the boats. Sometimes the customs officers would stand near the High Lights above the quay and watch the vessels, six deep below at the west quay, throughout the night. They may see a crew member leave a vessel with a bag and catch the chap at the top of the stairs rising from the quay to find he was carrying cigarettes to sell locally. One cunning ploy was if a crew member had broken an arm or leg while at sea, they were brought to the fish quay and taken off to go to hospital. Someone else from their fishing vessel would accompany them to hospital carrying a black bin liner, ostensibly of clothes and personal possessions of the injured party, "but often full of fags to sell," Rob remembers.

The author wished to include a photograph here which is visible on the Flikr website. Unsuccessful attempts were made to contact the photographer while seeking permission to use the picture. The photograph is in black and white, taken in 1965 and shows some piled Polish salt or fish barrels on the west quay at North Shields fish quay. Here is an internet link to the photograph ... https://www.flickr.com/

photos/geordie_rover/1419683508/ Therefore the author has included one of his own photographs here – of the fish quay metalwork shaped to show herring girls (from earlier times) packing such barrels.

HERRING GIRLS AND FISH BARRELS
Fish quay metalwork, designed by artist Maureen Black, shows fisher girls (from years gone by) storing herrings in barrels with salt. Photographed on 19 May 1991

In the early days of these troubles with the Polish fishing vessels they used to discharge their barrels of fish to their mother ship offshore. The mother ship would make shuttle trips back to Poland with her barrels of herring, etc. This practice later changed so the Polish fishing vessels used North Shields fish quay as an open air barrel store. The factory ship would unload empty barrels at the start of the fishing season and take away the full ones at the end of the season. There could be as many as 5,000 – 7,000 barrels of herring to take away once the fishing season concluded. Each barrel was marked with a number and it was not unknown for one to be filled with cigarettes. Such a barrel would eventually disappear off the quay! Empty barrels would be loaded onto fishing vessels at the quay as and when they were required during the season. There were however too many for them all to be opened and checked by the customs officers – so they would maintain a lookout and perform spot checks, but could not cover the quay 24 hours a day. Rob asked the Polish fishermen what happened in Poland with the contraband they were smuggling if the border guards found the goods. In Poland the guards were armed and could in theory shoot the fishermen. The reply that came from these fishermen was that they dumped half their contraband and while the guards were scrabbling for it the fishermen made a run for it. "Whether there is any truth in this I don't know, but this is what they used to say," said Rob. At that time the fish quay premises and businesses gutted, cleaned and packed fish after the British boats returned from their fishing trips of several days. These foreign vessels were following the fish around the shores of Britain.

Four HM Customs launches based on the river Tyne, and possibly in the period 1960 - 1963, were as follows:

- HMCL *Argus* a 55ft launch in service 1938 -1963 Tyne
- HMCL *Despatch* a 54ft launch in service 1955 - 1973 Tyne
- HMCL *Eider* a 36ft launch in service 1952 - 1963 Tyne
- HMCL *Mallard* a 36ft launch in service 1952 - 1965 Tyne

So Rob may have worked on some of these vessels.

After working on the river Tyne with HM Customs & Excise during 1960 - 1963, Rob carried out further roles with the service. Following an initial period of six to eight years as 'waterguard' staff, assistant preventive officers sat written examinations and attended interviews to become a preventive officer – gaining promotion from their assistant preventive officer role. Preventive officers may be located further afield – for example large numbers of Rob's colleagues went to Heathrow airport (during a

HMCL ARGUS
One of the customs launches Rob worked on from North Shields.
Photographed at Lowestoft, ca.1968. Photo courtesy of The Philip
Simons Collection

time of expansion), while others worked at Dover and Southampton during the summer seasons. Many preventive officers eventually gravitated to their formative home areas. Rob left the uniformed side of his job in late 1963 to carry out further duties. Such work was in landing and shipping cargos, breweries, distilleries, betting & gaming and general excise. He carried out these duties in northeast England, Skye, Orkney and the Highlands of Scotland. In the early 1970s he gained experience as an oils officer at the former *Esso* terminal on Howdon Road, North Shields, though his office was the then Custom House in Clive Street. This latter building (now demolished) was later occupied by John Lilley & Gillie Ltd, supplier of nautical instruments and equipment as well as charts. In the mid-1980s Rob carried out VAT and drug investigations for five and a half years in London. HM Customs & Excise provided Rob with a very varied and interesting career and he states that "If you did not like one type of work you could change to another." Although people now may receive a better general education than Rob and his cohorts during the 1950's and 1960's, he thinks his experiences, which included National Service and serving in the Merchant Navy with people from other areas, meant people travelled and mixed more. As an example of the usefulness of such experience he was able to train his colleagues on Tyneside after roles investigating fraud in London. Since his early time with HM Customs and Excise, such duties can now be more localised due to the expense of relocation.

His work used to be more physical than that of the modern day, which is often clerical and accountancy based. On modern huge cargo ships the crew complement may be as low as thirteen to move thousands of tons of material. In comparison, during his time with RFA *Tidereach* in the Merchant Navy he worked with a crew of 90 to 100 strong (though this figure was higher than normal, as refuelling at sea was quite labour-intensive and specialised).

Of his work on the river Tyne, Rob says "It was a wonderful place to be." Now retired, he continues to enjoy life with his wife Anne on Tyneside. He cannot believe how quiet the river is nowadays compared to when he worked at North Shields.

LAUNCH OF *RFA TIDEREACH*
Launch on the Tyne at the Wallsend Yard of Swan Hunter & Wigham Richardson, 1954. Photograph courtesy of Tyne and Wear Archives (Reference DS.SWH/4/PH/4/1847/5)

ORKNEY
Islands, sea and sky, 22 July 1993

SPEYSIDE
The River Spey at Boat of Garten,
Scottish Highlands, with the
snow-speckled Cairngorm massif
in the distance, 27 May 1997

ISLE OF SKYE
The Quiraing, Trotternish Ridge,
Skye, 13 June 1984

Rob worked with HM Customs & Excise on the Isle of Skye, Orkney and in the
Highlands of Scotland during 1966 - 1967.

Roy Elliott

Tynemouth & North Shields lad and
fisherman from 1980 to present

Roy was born in Knott's Flats, Tynemouth,
just a short walk down the bank to the fish
quay. He used to live two doors from Jackie
Weatherstone, thirty years his senior, who
lived with his own parents and brother.
When Roy was seven years old he first
went to sea, with Jackie as skipper, on
Karen Obbekaer (BCK 134), "Jackie used
to shout and bawl … a bit of a bully! We
were only young!" remembered Roy. "He
used to say 'You owe me a pound!' Seeing
Jackie at his store on the quay now he sits
like a mouse – quite different!" Roy smiled
as he recounted this tale. His parents knew
Jackie's and they realised their young son
would be safe with this fisherman neighbour
from along the corridor. As a boy he gained experience at weekends, on occasional
day trips, trawling and fishing for prawns. "All the lads from Knott's Flats went to the
fish quay", recounted Roy, and it was no surprise that he took things further.

PORTRAIT
Roy at the fish quay with the New High Light on the bank top behind, 25 May 2012

KNOTT'S FLATS IN THE SNOW
These homes enjoy a Tyne river mouth view on a snowy afternoon, 14 January 2013

Roy attended Linskill High School, North Shields, and on leaving in 1980 went fishing straight away on different local boats … for salmon in the summer, trawling in the winter and gill netting. One of the boats he worked on during this period was coble *Golden City* on which Roy fished with owner Peter Henderson. This coble was kept at Cullercoats and would be hauled up and down with a tractor to and from the hard-standing in the bottom of the bay. Roy and Peter took turns to drive the tractor on which the exhaust pipe exited above the water line. They fished for salmon on a licence belonging to Jackie Weatherstone, at one time, when they were allowed to fish for this species at night. So a day crew would go out with one boat followed by a night crew on another boat and they would hand over the salmon fishing licence tags as the crew changed over. There were two tags: a yellow one which was displayed on the boat and another, perhaps of a different colour, for attachment to the net. Another coble he was on for a few months was *Dayspring*, owned by Ray Mundy. They fished for salmon at night and with pots during the day. In those days they brought up mostly lobsters in their pots, but they did not fish them as intensively as he does nowadays. After two or three years of short-term boat experiences, such as with *Golden City* and *Dayspring*, he settled into a two year spell as crew member

A FULL GUT
Karen Obbekaer (BCK 134) in a packed Gut at the fish quay, 27 September 1987

on *Conduan* (BCK 4) between 1983 and 1985. Norrie Morse was skipper / owner of this vessel on which Roy experienced summer fishing trips of 4-7 days at a time, while in the winter they fished on day trips from North Shields for prawns. In the summer his trips on *Conduan* would take him "up to 150 miles" from the harbour. For instance they would steam 50-60 miles off, but if the catch was poor they would steam in the dark to a new spot for another day's fishing and so on. "If the fishing was okay we just stopped handy," Roy explained, but often this fishing boat covered further distance overnight in search of good grounds.

ALL AT SEA
Roy Elliott (right) with Tommy Taylor, aboard North Shields coble *Ocean Pride* (SN 139) while salmon fishing, ca. 1982 - 1983. Photograph from Roy's family album

CONDUAN IN THE TYNE
Decked out for the fish quay festival, *Conduan* (BCK 4) passes the quayside, 9 May 1987

Experiencing violent sea sickness at first, it would take Roy some time to get his sea legs and, when moving to a different large boat, it may be a couple of days before he settled. He was sick as a young lad of seven on his first trip to sea, "But when you came through the piers and saw Knott's Flats up above you would be fine ... it was a great feeling!"

Following *Conduan*, he spent eleven years (1985 - 1996) on *Silver Echo* (LH 453), owned by Kenneth Foster, fishing from North Shields. For the last five years of the eleven he was skipper. In the summer some trips would last two to three days, but mostly *Silver Echo* fished on day trips and Roy continued salmon fishing, in season, on this vessel. "When salmon fishing now you are not allowed to fish inside of one mile from south of Marconi Point (Cullercoats) or beyond five miles out," he explained to me, "And the hours are regulated." Roy told me she was a comfortable boat of something over forty feet in length with a crew of three in his first two or three years with her, reducing to two handed afterwards. When they hauled the trawl net both men would be on deck ... one forward operating the machinery to haul while the other was at the stern clipping and unclipping the trawl doors, etc. They would land their catches daily and Roy could not remember any real breakdowns of gear during this eleven year period. Summer brought early morning starts of two or three o'clock, with later winter days commencing at half past six i.e. mainly fishing during daylight hours.

Owner Kenny Foster sold *Silver Echo* in 1996 and bought coble *Kerry Ann B*, which he owned for two years up to 1998 and Roy fished with her for salmon and with gill nets. Gill nets sit on the bottom of the sea bed, with floats along the top line lifting the net in the water. In 1998 he started to fish from Blyth on a small trawl boat called *Margaret Kerr*, owned and skippered by Davy Kerr. The two of them fished together on this vessel until 2002 – trawling, fishing for salmon and also with pots.

In 2002 Roy bought coble *Anne Lynn* (HL 85) and steamed her to her new home port of North Shields from Hartlepool. He owned and fished with *Anne Lynn* for four years ... with pots and gill netting up to two miles off. Roy explained that, with such a net, the time when it catches fish is when the tide is either at low water or high when the currents slow and consequently stop pushing the net over in one direction

SILVER ECHO
Blue-hulled *Silver Echo* (LH 453) rests in the snowy Gut alongside *Sovereign* (HL 165) and *Castle Dawn*, 25 December 1985

QUITE A CATCH!
Roy with a tope (a shark species) aboard *Sophie Louise* while fishing from North Shields. Roy was a crew member for about a year in the early to mid-1990s. Photograph from Roy's family album

KERRY ANN B
Sturdy coble *Kerry Ann B* (SN 168) at North Shields fish quay, 16 January 1988

(either inshore or offshore). This is called "Tiding the gear," Roy told me indicating a change of tide is when best to catch fish. "Gill nets are meant to hang like curtains," he said, "Different times of year, weather and tide determine where you put the pots and nets." He has strings of thirty pots and when bad weather is forecast may shift them two miles further out to stop them from getting damaged and washed onto the shore … large boulders can be moved about in heavy seas and flatten pots. "After hard weather it can be like Whacky Races – everybody trying to get their pots into the best position again!" There are no fixed positions for the pots and other cobles are competing for the good spots.

ANNE LYNN
Coble *Anne Lynn* (HL 85) rests at the fish quay with the New Low Light behind, 20 April 2005

Fishermen at one time were allowed to shoot seals which were eating salmon caught within their nets, "It was called pest control," Roy informed me, and continued "If Jackie Weatherstone says he ever shot a seal he isn't telling the truth! If he pointed the gun over there," indicating in front, "… the shot would hit the water behind him. He was not the greatest shot!"

RE-PAINTING
Roy's coble *Stacey E*, during her annual re-paint at Royal Quays boatyard, 10 May 2012

During 2006 Roy purchased coble *KJB* from Jackie and promptly renamed her to *Stacey E* (SN 332), after his daughter, costing around £70 for the change of name. He takes his coble out of the water at the Royal Quays Marina (just upriver from the fish quay) annually for a fortnight to re-paint and carry out maintenance. With *Stacey E* he fishes alone with gill nets and for salmon in the season. He also generally works 300 to 500 pots on lines of thirty – each pot is spaced by about thirty feet, and each with its own six foot length of rope. The 'slave hauler' on his coble hauls up the main rope with the pots and Roy regulates its speed so he can lift the pots aboard in turn ready for re-baiting and shooting back into the water later – one at a time. As the pots are hauled the coble moves forwards, pulled along the full length of the rope by the action of the slave hauler after picking up the rope from the dahn at the start of a line of pots. As well as lobsters in the pots he catches velvet crabs … "they only appeared [in our pots] about twenty years ago, but have multiplied dramatically since then."

GOING FISHING
Roy leaves the fish quay manoeuvring the rudder aboard *Stacey E* (SN 332), mid-morning on 29 May 2011

"In the summer you could get four or five lobsters in one pot, but in the winter you might only get six lobsters all day." A gauge is used to check the length of the lobster carapace and, of perhaps 600 lobsters caught on a good summer's day Roy may return 75-80% undersized ones to the sea. The carapace is measured from the eye to the rear of the head. Berries (or eggs) may be found at any time of year on the underside of lobsters, Roy told me, but they are discarded during processing once the shellfish are landed. He sells his lobsters directly to Moir Seafood, owned and run by Paul Dowse. When he owned *Anne Lynn* Roy used to sell his catch to a business called Northumbria Crab (next to Dock Road and opposite the Wolsington House public house, North Shields). This business was owned by the late Alan Laurie who used to own and fish vessels *Phaeton I* (SN 44) and *Helga Risager* (WA 45) from North Shields.

Roy has passed various compulsory courses for his job including: sea survival, radio, safety awareness, first aid, risk assessment and fire fighting. Some are basic training

ROY AND HIS POTS
On the afternoon of Tuesday 27 November 2012 Roy was working at the fish quay – mending holes in his lobster pots

courses with no expiry date, some were taken at South Shields in a classroom and at the Derby Street baths in that town, for example sea survival was taken at the baths. He has repeated certain courses at the Linskill Centre, Linskill Terrace, North Shields, while he took the radio ticket at the RNMDSF, Union Quay (now a restaurant), on the fish quay.

In May 2005 for a couple of weeks a tame small cormorant followed Roy's coble while he was fishing on the sea off Tynemouth and Cullercoats. This was not an immature bird since Roy said it had no white on the chest. Every day it came close to the boat and Roy would cut some strips of fish, which he was using for bait, for the cormorant – which it would come to take as Roy held them out for the bird. The cormorant would dive as gulls came close to try to take its food. The

EARLY MORNING CORMORANTS
Cormorants stand at dawn on Lloyd's jetty, beside the fish quay, 11 November 2012

bird would also fly alongside the boat as he steamed inshore … Roy said "Like you see on nature programmes on the TV" – when birds are filmed in flight alongside a flying camera.

Roy fitted a re-conditioned engine to *Stacey E* in 2010, "It vibrates at low speed, so you need to keep a few revs on." It is a marine-ised Ford wagon engine – which was altered so it uses sea water sucked in for cooling the fresh water that in turn cools the engine. The warmed sea water exits from the boat and more cool water is sucked in to continue the cycle. His boat's fresh-water tank is made from brass and the sea water runs in pipes through this … so cooling the fresh water. Roy may purchase a newer fishing boat in the future.

GUTTING THE CATCH
Roy guts his day's catch of cod aboard *Stacey E*. The gulls have come for the left overs, mid-afternoon on 8 January 2011

Stuart Brown

Tynemouth lifeboat volunteer from 1973 to 1996

Stuart, born in North Shields, has been personally associated with North Shields fish quay for over fifty years, from an early age, and used to bunk off Sunday School at the age of eight to go there and catch crabs. He was meant to be attending at the Methodist Church in Howard Street, but would escape to lower hooks baited with fish over the side of the quay to attract crabs and come back home later stinking of fish. He reminisced that there were hundreds of trawlers in those days, but the numbers have died off since.

Stuart served his time at Daniel's Garage, on Albion Road, over the road from Turnbull's funeral Directors – there are still garages there … Tynemouth Motor Company and Central Motors (and Davidson's Garage in earlier years). He used to repair and maintain the work vehicles belonging to George Purdy on the fish quay. The Purdy business owned a land rover that towed fishing boats, resting in the river, along the quayside – moving them around. Stuart recalled George Griggson who was a ship's husband and worked for Purdy's which also carried supplies for the fishing vessels. Freeth's was another quayside business that provided boat provisions and also sold fishing hooks. Stuart would buy a ha'penny hook from Freeth's to catch sprats and sometimes purchased the more expensive 'goldie', made from brass, for a penny.

PORTRAIT
Stuart at the lifeboat station with Collingwood's monument, Lloyd's jetty and Tynemouth north pier & lighthouse behind, 6 May 2012

In those days there were thousands of sprats in the river due to the vast numbers of herring that were landed here. They were landed in large baskets that were filled to overflowing and the topmost fish would often slip and fall into the river as the baskets were being offloaded and the sprats in the river fed on the dead herrings. Stuart's mother used to make a dish called 'Mopped Herring' which is a filleted and rolled herring, in the shape of a mop, which is then oven-cooked for a few minutes. Stuart's mother would warn him to keep away from the boats at the quay as it was dangerous due to the fact that the very many cables mooring the boats were under high tension in the moving water and at times snapped causing injuries or even fatalities.

In his younger days he said it was possible to always get fish from the quay by asking "Can we have a fry?" Stuart said this has largely stopped with the price of cod now reaching about £8 a kilo. The Haddock Shop, which is the small dock between the riverside apartments called Dolphin Quays at the bottom of Bedford Street, was where fishing boats came for repairs when Stuart worked in the garage.

Stuart first became involved with Tynemouth lifeboat in the 1970s when living in Denwick Terrace, Tynemouth, next door to a house owned by the RNLI where the lifeboat mechanic lived. At first, before helping to crew a lifeboat, Stuart was winch-man in charge of lifeboat launches and recovery back into the lifeboat house. This was lifeboat *Tynesider* which used to be based at the fish quay sands where she was kept inside the lifeboat house from where she was launched into the river from

TYNESIDER LAUNCH
Lifeboat *Tynesider* launches into the Tyne from the lifeboat house slipway, North Shields fish quay. *Tynesider* served here during 1947 - 1979. Photograph courtesy of Tynemouth lifeboat station archives

a slipway. A two and a half inch thick cable was used to pull *Tynesider* backwards up the slipway and into the boat house. This required the lifeboat to be steadied by two wires, often in rolling water conditions, one from the pilot jetty (Lloyd's hailing station) and one from the government jetty. A whistle would be blown when the lifeboat was in line ready to be winched up the slipway with the keel running up the central groove. This was a skilful job and took Stuart some time to master in order to ensure the keel ran in the groove. In the boat house the lifeboat was held in place with a large two-piece hook at the rear of the vessel, half way up the stern. When the coxswain shouted "Slip" at a launch, Stuart would launch the lifeboat by knocking a pin out, allowing the hook to dissemble and the boat would glide down the slipway and make a spectacular splash as it entered the river, becoming almost completely submerged in water on entry. Stuart recalled Fred Arkley, a Tyne foy-boatman, who was also a lifeboat man; lifeboat helper and trainer Leonard Park; and other crew

CREW PHOTOGRAPH
At the lifeboat station, west quay, North Shields fish quay. *RNLB George and Olive Turner* (52-13) with some of her volunteer crew – including Stuart Brown (second from right, front), Trevor Fryer (right), Martin Kenny (up steps) and John Norris (standing tall at bottom of steps). Photograph courtesy of Tynemouth lifeboat station archives

members of the time including Trevor Fryer and Jimmy Crawshaw who ran the Bath Hotel in Tynemouth and was second coxswain on the *Tynesider*.

Fishing vessels often trawl up from the sea and land strange objects at the quay, for example a Spitfire engine. Stuart has a photograph of his young son on such an object retrieved from the seabed – a very large anchor. Following his service on *Tynesider*, Stuart progressed to the Barnett class lifeboat *Princess Alexandra* followed by the *George and Olive Turner* (Arun class lifeboat). When Stuart was involved with the *George and Olive Turner*, she was firstly berthed at Brigham's dock South Shields, before moving across to berth next to the ice factory on the west quay at North Shields fish quay. He also served on the inshore D class lifeboat for around ten years and would attend such incidents as children on airbeds floating out to sea and vessels sinking or on fire. Altogether Stuart was credited with 23 years as a volunteer with the lifeboat service in his retirement Certificate of Service from the RNLI committee of

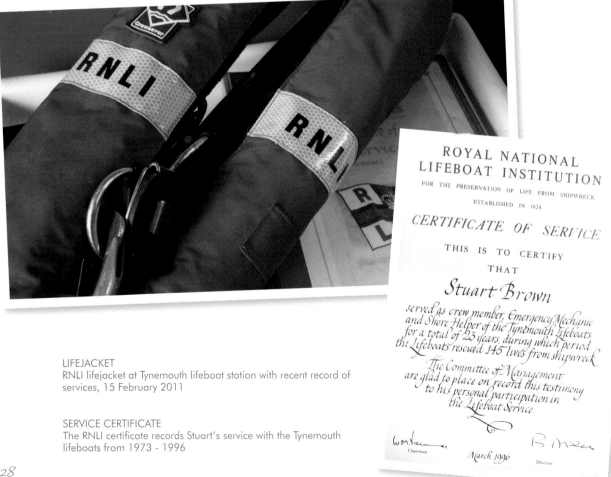

LIFEJACKET
RNLI lifejacket at Tynemouth lifeboat station with recent record of services, 15 February 2011

SERVICE CERTIFICATE
The RNLI certificate records Stuart's service with the Tynemouth lifeboats from 1973 - 1996

management in March 1996, having 'served as crew member, emergency mechanic and shore helper of the Tynemouth lifeboats …'

A very notable service for Stuart was when he was helmsman on the inshore boat with two other crew members and went to the rescue of a Cullercoats coble *John Dory* on 22 February 1981. The conditions were cold with a SE force 6 wind, snow squalls and heavy seas. The *John Dory*, 16 feet in length and made from fibreglass, had been launched with four men aboard, an angling party, and capsized throwing them into the water about 100 to 150 yards from the Cullercoats harbour entrance. Fisherman Geoff Nugent (father of Michael, who features in this book) alerted the coastguards at 10:13 a.m. that Sunday morning when the men were plunged into the freezing waters. Geoff had been unable to launch his own coble for several days, due to "atrocious" conditions, and was reported to say "Even the most experienced fishermen would not have gone out on that day." Cullercoats lifeboat station was closed, opening only in the summer at that time. The helicopter was called and the Tynemouth inshore lifeboat launched at 10:27 a.m. reaching the casualty at 10:40. One boy swam ashore and was taken to hospital. The helicopter had picked up two men from the water, both critical, and one apparently dead, by 10:39 a.m., and the winch man gave heart massage and mouth to mouth resuscitation. The helicopter pilot could not see the fourth man, so flew to the Newcastle Royal Victoria Infirmary with the rescued pair while the ILB searched for the fourth man at rock ends and in channels. The coble was foundering on the north side of Cullercoats north pier. Stuart brought the lifeboat round three or four times at a channel where they thought the fourth man from the coble may be, to attempt a rescue, but on the final attempt the waves flicked the lifeboat over spilling Stuart and his crew into the sea and trapping crew man Graeme Boyd underneath. Third crew man Jimmy Griffiths swam to his aid, lifted the side and helped pull out Graeme. Then Jimmy was swept, on the back of the lifeboat, inshore and onto rocks. The helicopter quickly returned to the scene from Newcastle and managed to rescue Stuart, who had by now been washed some distance to sea, and Graeme in turn from the water to land them on the beach. Both were taken to hospital. Stuart was detained in Tynemouth Jubilee Infirmary for quite a while suffering from hypothermia and an arm injury. In the rush to launch, his typhoon dry suit had not been zipped up, so when he was thrown into the sea it soon filled with water and dragged him down (causing him to almost drown). The rescue quickly featured on the front page of many newspapers the next day – both local (The Journal) and national (the Times). The Times article included a photo of the helicopter winching up a casualty from the sea. The fourth man from the coble was

SERVICE TO *JOHN DORY*
This rescue off Cullercoats in atrocious conditions led to the Tynemouth inshore lifeboat overturning and the consequent rescue of two crew members (including Stuart) from the sea by RAF helicopter, 22 February 1981. The photograph shows the Sea King rescue helicopter landing a man on the beach after he was plucked from the sea. In the background the inshore lifeboat, which had overturned, is pulled ashore. Picture courtesy of ncjMedia Ltd

picked up dead by the RAF helicopter, trapped three feet underwater by seaweed and rope from the boat, and two weeks later in hospital a second, rescued, man died. The four men from the coble had been wearing oilskins and wellingtons, but not their life-jackets; this clothing therefore pulled them down in the water.

Stuart received a certificate from the RNLI for his service as a member of the crew of the D class inflatable lifeboat during the rescue of nine people from the motor boat *Blue Fin* off Trow Rocks, South Shields on 11 April 1982. *Blue Fin* was subsequently wrecked on the rocks. Trevor Fryer was helmsman during this rescue and received thanks from the Institution inscribed on vellum and was awarded a gold medal for bravery by Tyne and Wear County Council (refer to Trevor Fryer's section in this book for further details).

This is to certify that
Stuart Brown
*was a member of the crew
of the Tynemouth D class inflatable life-boat
and took part in the service
which was recognised by the
Committee of Management
by the Thanks of the Institution inscribed on vellum
being accorded to Helmsman
Trevor Fryer
when on the 11th April, 1982,
the life-boat rescued nine people
from the motor boat 'Blue Fin'
which had broken down off Trow Point
and was subsequently wrecked on the rocks
in a strong northerly wind and a rough breaking sea.*

DIRECTOR & SECRETARY

RNLI CERTIFICATE
Marking Stuart's involvement in the *Blue Fin* rescue of 11 April 1982

RNLI CROWN AND ANCHOR
From the header of Stuart's certificate for his involvement in the rescue from *Blue Fin*

On 12 January 1986 Stuart was a member of the crew of the inshore lifeboat with Jimmy Griffiths and helmsman Trevor Fryer when three children had been cut off by the tide south of Marsden Rock. Refer to Trevor Fryer's section in this book for further details.

On 27 May 1986 Cullercoats fishing coble *James Denyer*, with two men aboard, drifted onto the Black Middens in a westerly force 8 gale after suffering engine failure. A letter with grateful thanks, from the RNLI Chief of Operations, was received by Stuart for his and Trevor Fryer's efforts to 'ensure a safe and satisfactory outcome to this service.' Stuart's letter records 'It is noted that throughout this two hour service, in storm conditions during which the D class lifeboat (D-280) was frequently filled

by breaking seas, as helmsman you carried out your duties in the finest traditions of the lifeboat service. As a consequence of your actions, the coble was successfully refloated with assistance from the Arun class lifeboat (*George and Olive Turner*), and the coble escorted safely back to Tynemouth fish quays.' The service took place in the early afternoon. Helmsman Trevor requested, approaching low water, the Arun lifeboat to make a 'close pass or two' to see if her wake could re-float the coble, but this was to no avail. Then 40 minutes after low water (LW was at 13:01 BST) the coble was pulled clear. Current Tynemouth lifeboat coxswain Michael Nugent recalls following the *James Denyer* upriver, after the incident, aboard Shields coble *Ocean Pride*.

Stuart's grandfather (Warmington), on his mother's side, was involved as a fisherman with the old sailing trawlers from North Shields. Stuart's father was George Matthew Brown, a slater and tiler, who worked on the roof of the Plaza at Tynemouth sea front. The Plaza, previously called the 'Winter Palace', was built in the late nineteenth century and its roof contained asbestos, a contributory factor

RNLB GEORGE AND OLIVE TURNER
The Arun class lifeboat passes the fish quay, heading upriver. She was the Tynemouth all-weather lifeboat during
1980 - 1999. Photograph courtesy of Tynemouth lifeboat station archives

in Stuart's father's death from asbestosis. Stuart worked for George Angus & Co.
Ltd, off Tynemouth Coast Road (A1058) at Wallsend, for many years – concluding
as factory quality control auditor before his retirement from employment in 1999.
Stuart's wife Liz is a member of St Columba's Church (North Shields), the 'Silver
Singers' and of Tynemouth Operatic Society for over 50 years. The couple enjoy
caravanning in France and previously using Stuart's small angling boat on trips to
northwest Scotland.

Stuart's wife's father was Gordon Turnbull, an active member of Tynemouth
Photographic Society from around 1937 until he died in 2000. The couple have
three lovely black and white prints by Gordon hanging alongside their staircase
at home – 'Shell Shock' (featuring a little glass swan ornament and broken egg
shell), one taken at the fish quay with a hanging fishing net in the foreground and
a third photo of Liz in the rain as a young girl. Gordon held such positions as:
president of Northern Counties Photographic Federation (1952 - 1954), president

of the Photographic Alliance of Great Britain (1963 - 1965), president (thrice) and secretary of Tynemouth Photographic Society.

RNLI HERALDIC EMBLEM
From the top of Stuart's Certificate of Service recording his 23 years as a volunteer with the Tynemouth lifeboats

LIFEBOAT STATION SIGN
At Tynemouth lifeboat station, 23 February 2008

Tommy Bailey (senior)

North Shields lad and fisherman from 1958 - 2010

Tommy was born in 1943 at 155 Church Street, North Shields. Church Street no longer exists, but was between where Linskill Street and Dockwray Square stand today above the fish quay. Tommy's father, James, had been a fisherman, as had a number of previous local family generations. James Bailey had a diesel fishing boat *Girl Irene* (SN 19) built in Banff in 1957. The original crew were James Bailey and his four sons James (the eldest), Alan, Tommy and Colin (the youngest) and this was the first boat on which Tommy worked after leaving school at the age of 15. *Girl Irene* was a dual purpose vessel, used for trawling and as a seine net boat, and would go fishing on day trips from Shields. "I enjoyed it," Tommy said. "Suppose you marry the sea," his wife Hazel commented as they sat together. Father James Bailey was owner and skipper of *Girl Irene*, owning her for six years before she was sold, after which Tommy and his brothers split up and went to work on different boats from North Shields. He and his brothers became mates and skippers on other local boats and they all then started to work for North Shields fishing companies Richard Irvin and William Purdy. Tommy's eldest brother James ended up as skipper of the *Lindisfarne* (BCK 147).

After two years with *Girl Irene*, from 1958 - 1960, Tommy joined a new fishing vessel called *Condowan* (KY 247). He joined this new boat on her maiden voyage

LINDISFARNE
The wheelhouse of fishing vessel *Lindisfarne* (BCK 147) at North Shields fish quay, 11 October 1987

CONDOWAN
Fishing vessel *Condowan* (KY 247), photographed from the fish quay with a snowy South Shields scene behind, 28 December 1985

from Anstruther, where she was built, to North Shields, stopping at Eyemouth en route as there was a south-easterly gale blowing. North Shields man Jackie Dowse was skipper and part owner of *Condowan* and she was crewed by Jackie's brother, Norman Dowse, a Scotsman called Mick Hughes, Arthur Hunter (Jackie Dowse's brother-in-law), Charlie Brown and Tommy Bailey. "I did not make much money on her," Tommy stated, "but the skipper was a proper gentleman." He went on, "The crew used to be paid on what they could do … splice, mend nets, etc. Now fishermen get equal shares. So in the past it used to take time until you all got the same wage." It must have taken time for the men to learn these new skills. Aboard *Condowan* for two years Tommy was a deckhand and used to pull in the nets, take watch and help shoot the fishing gear. The fishing trips were between two and four days in length and they would go anchor fishing, seining and trawling. Skipper Jackie would steam the vessel perhaps between 60 and 160 miles in different directions from east to southeast and northeast. They would fish at different locations, depending on time of year, in order to vary the species caught.

RICHARD IRVIN BUILDING
One of the buildings (now demolished) of Richard Irvin & Sons Ltd, Union Road, North Shields fish quay, 30 September 2001

On leaving *Condowan*, Tommy "signed onto the Richard Irvin trawlers," with his friend Stanton Clay and started on vessel *Abergeldie* (A 174) – a coal-burning steam boat with a crew of eleven. He signed on as a deckie / trimmer shovelling coal since this was a steam trawler, while Stanton signed on as a deckhand. The boat would travel on trips of eight to ten days and he continued this work for a few years, "The kids hardly knew him in those days," Hazel said of their four children. After a spell with *Abergeldie*, there followed a period of changing among different trawlers for Irvin and he spent a few years between vessels *Ben Vurie* (SN 33), *Ben Strome* (SN 95) and *Ben Tork*. These were "big trips" and took Tommy to the Faeroes, Iceland and Bailey sea areas. This was deep water trawling for cod, haddock, coley (also known as blackjack) and many other species. The author asked if Tommy could see other fishing vessels when fishing in such remote places and he replied, "There were many boats all around when you were fishing … they would all stick together and follow each other."

Following this trawling period throughout the 1960s Tommy went to Grimsby and sailed on an anchor boat called *Crathie Top* (GY 394), originally a Danish vessel, skippered by James Drury. Their fishing trips lasted a few days and when not fishing he would take the train home to North Shields. He spent two years fishing from Grimsby like this, then "came back to Shields," which would have been in the early 1970s, when he was living with his family in Waterville Road.

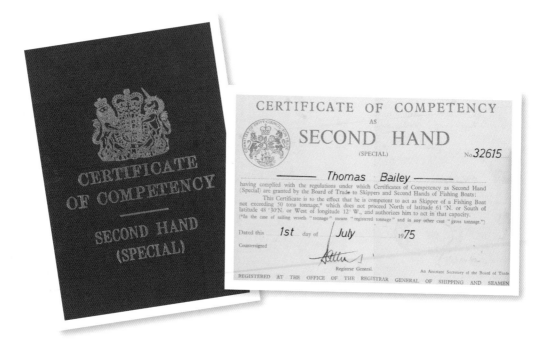

SKIPPER'S TICKET
Tommy's 'Second Hand Special' certificate, granted on 1 July 1975. This allowed Tommy to act as skipper of vessels up to 50 tons

Then Tommy came ashore and in 1975 took his skipper's ticket at South Shields, sitting the examinations with Richard Leighton ('Dicky'), one-time owner of the New Dolphin public house on the fish quay. "I worked on loads of boats after that, mostly from Eyemouth," Tommy remarked. His skipper's ticket, or Second Hand Special, allowed him to skipper vessels up to 50 tons and act as mate on vessels above this size. During this next phase as a skipper he travelled on fishing trips of three to four days duration from Eyemouth and would be brought home by car or minibus to Shields on Sundays since a few of the fishermen were from here. From Eyemouth he worked on boats owned and skippered by the Moodie brothers. These vessels were

Sharona (LH 263, on which Tommy was mate), *Sharon Dawn* and *Rose of Sharon III* (LH 56) … on the latter two boats Tommy was deckhand. In 1980 he joined a Pittenweem boat called *Ina McBain* (KY 385) and was based with her for a few years fishing from Pittenween and North Shields as deckhand and skipper. Tommy recalled that 1981 was the year of the first North Shields fish quay festival, run informally by the fishermen and their families at that time, and during the festival he was aboard *Ina McBain* – decked out with flags. In 1986 Tommy hurt his back, weakened from years at sea. "The sea got the blame," he and his wife Hazel agreed. He then "pottered about" until his oldest son, also called Tommy, bought a coble in 1996.

LARGE HAUL OF COD
Tommy and his son Andy aboard coble *Eleanor Dawson* (BK 17) alongside the fish quay – with a record haul of cod, ca. 1996. Photograph courtesy of Thomas Bailey

ROYAL SOVEREIGN
This was Tommy's coble (SN 356) at North Shields from 2004 - 2010. Photograph taken on 10 April 2005

This coble was called *Eleanor Dawson* (BK 17), which the two Tommys (senior and junior) worked together, using pots and nets inside of six miles out, "We used to help each other out," he said. In 1996 Tommy landed North Shields' best catch of fish from a coble … 35 boxes of cod weighing 280 stones. Later *Eleanor Dawson* was decommissioned and Tommy thinks she went to Redcar. Tommy Bailey senior then bought another coble in 2004, *Royal Sovereign* (SN 356), which he owned until 2010 when he officially retired. With *Royal Sovereign*, based at North Shields, Tommy also worked pots and nets inshore. During late August 2008, Tommy told the author, when two and a half miles out at sea working his pots he saw a minke whale quite

TOMMY AND HIS POTS
Aboard *Royal Sovereign*, North Shields fish quay, 3 May 2009

LOBSTER AND CRAB POTS
Tommy's pots at the fish quay, 10 April 2005

close, heading south and lazing in the sea. On Friday 19 September 2008 Tommy emptied his 60 self-baiting crab and lobster pots. This produced a good catch of two boxes of crabs, weighing seven stones, and 16 lobsters. He also said there was a school of eight to ten porpoises offshore on that occasion when 2.5 miles out.

Tommy's eldest brother James did well as skipper of *Lindisfarne*, from North Shields, and died at the age of 60 in 1995. He was a good friend of North Shields skipper Cliff Ellis. His brother Alan left North Shields around 1973 - 1975 and married a Scottish girl from Buckie, moving to live there and fish for most of his life – he is now retired. Tommy's brother Colin was a part-time fisherman who also worked at various factories and businesses including Tyne Brand and British Ropes. As well as being a fisherman, Tommy's father James was a net mender and ended up as watchman for the North Shields fish quay boats. Tommy and his brothers all learnt (from their father) how to mend nets, a job they were able to do ashore. When Tommy's father came ashore for a spell and, when working at Smiths Docks, "He was on the dock bottom when a lad slipped the anchor which fell and crushed his leg." With the compensation from this accident James had bought *Girl Irene*, the first boat Tommy had fished upon. Tommy concluded … telling the author that "All fishermen have a spell ashore, but they all go back!"

BRINGING HER IN
Royal Sovereign is steered on the river Tyne by skipper Thomas Bailey (senior) to her berth in the fish quay Gut,
13 September 2009

MINKE WHALE
Tommy saw a minke whale in late August 2008 when out with his coble from North Shields. The photograph was taken from St Kilda, Scotland, 22 July 2009 © Ian Fisher

HARBOUR PORPOISES
Photographed at Faxafloi bay, Reykjavik, Iceland on 3 June 2009. Tommy Bailey saw a school of porpoises when out checking his pots in September 2008. © Chiara Giulia Bertulli / Faxafloi Cetacean Research, University of Iceland

BOX OF CRABS
Landed by fisherman and lifeboat coxswain Michael Nugent at the fish quay on 16 June 2013

Tony (Anthony) Asiamah

North Shields born, wholesale and retail fish merchant

Tony's father came to North Shields from Ghana just after World War II to work at Ellington colliery as a miner. He died from emphysema, brought on by coal mining, when Tony was quite young (less than ten years of age). In Ghana, Daniel Martin Asiamah had worked with the Ghanaian Air Force as a tank driver. He met his wife, Norah Todd (born in 1928), at North Shields, and they lived on the Meadowell estate. Tony is the youngest of four brothers … he also has four sisters, two of whom are younger than him. None of his siblings work in the fishing industry, but all are still based on Tyneside. Following the death of his father, Tony's mother brought up the family. Tony recalled that, "Things were hard … had no money … life was like that for almost everyone on the Meadowell." Tony attended Western Board Junior School at Penman Street, North Shields. He then progressed to Ralph Gardner School and left at sixteen years of age.

At the age of sixteen, on leaving school, Tony came down to the fish quay to look for a job. He first asked at the Bowers fish merchant business and was offered a job straight away. Bowers was based just behind the New Low Light, where currently there is a patch of grass beside Clifford's Fort wall. Here Tony worked on a Baader machine – this was a filleting machine that took the heads off fish; the fish then dropped and were split in two. Bowers dealt with cod and Tony worked here for between six months and a year. Wilf Kay owned and ran the business with his wife and son Dave. Tony recalled there were about six staff during his period there. The premises were right next to the fish quay market where Wilf went to buy cod. The staff would process the fish and a wagon came at the end of the day to take their products away. Bowers also had a big freezer and the staff made laminated blocks of minced fish for fish cakes and fish fingers. The laps that had been cut off the cod were sent away, minced and returned to Bowers where they were put into small blocks to freeze. A wagon came to take the frozen blocks away for the fish trade. After Wilf Kay died in later years Bowers closed.

FILLETING MACHINE
Dave Kay loads the filleting machine with codling, Bowers fish merchant, North Shields fish quay, 1980.
© Nick Hedges

FILLETING CODLING
Tony fillets codling at the business of John Ellis, North Shields fish quay. Photograph ca. 1971. © Brian Long

After his spell with Bowers, Tony became employed by fish merchant John Ellis in 1971 on the fish quay – receiving a higher wage than at his first job which had been full-time. John bought fish from the morning market, which he still does today, to take to his store … at that time located beside the former quay or harbour master's home and office which is opposite John's current premises. Here the filleters would cut the fish for local trade i.e. wet fish shops and for wholesale supply to fish and chip shops. At that time John Ellis employed four fish filleters and it was here that Tony learnt to fillet fish. He started with whiting. This was a cheap product which, if damaged would not cost the business a lot of money. As his filleting skills improved, Tony progressed to cutting cod, haddock, flatfish and everything else besides. He would start work at five o'clock in the morning and usually end at lunch time or just after. If there were a lot of fish to work on, John would take his staff on the back of a wagon into North Shields for a lunchtime Chinese meal, before continuing the shift afterwards. Tony worked on a bench with John Ellis who taught him tricks of the trade, such as handling and weighing fish and selling to customers. John taught Tony a lot about the trade and encouraged him to get involved. John Ellis had a 'poppa'. This had a Lister engine at the front and a flat back with a steel plate above the axle and wheels. Boxes of fish were loaded from the market onto the steel back plate and brought to John's store. As well as filleting, Tony would drive the poppa, moving the fish boxes around. When Tony passed his driving test at the age of 17 his employer John Ellis gave him five pounds to celebrate. He worked with John for three years and was then offered a position with better pay at Walkers Fish Merchants.

Tony started with Walkers Fish Merchants (Vita House) at the fish quay in 1974. Walkers was run by Tommy Mcwhinnie, a big wholesale fish merchant who processed fish and employed four filleters at the time. All the fish was bought from the quay market and processed daily. Tony started at six o'clock in the morning and sometimes would not finish until twelve hours later. The business had a delivery van and supplied hotels, restaurants, wet fish shops, fried fish shops, and many good local businesses. Some of the wet fish shops they supplied were located in Jarrow and South Shields. Walkers processed all sorts of fish, including lots of flatfish – such as plaice and lemon sole … "Lots of everything," confirmed Tony, "it was a very busy place." Tony got to know the delivery round and drove the Sherpa vans if a driver was off sick or on holiday. In the back of the vans the fish was transported in plastic containers to colleges, schools, hospitals, "all sorts of places." A delivery run may take three to four hours and sometimes Tony would be required to make two delivery runs in a day. During all of the time spent with Walkers he was a fish filleter.

Tony had played football at school, representing Ralph Gardener's (Chirton) and also North Shields 'Town'. In the 1970s he was a semi-professional footballer, while

YELLOW 'POPPA'
Tony carried boxes of fish on the poppa from the market to fish merchant John Ellis for processing. Beside Tony stands co-worker Alec Latimer. Photograph ca. 1972. © Brian Long

MARKET ACTIVITY
From left: Fish merchants Dennis Bell and Tommy Mcwhinnie (Walkers Fish Merchants) with Richard Irvin auctioneer George Harvey, fish quay market, 1980. © Nick Hedges

still working at Walkers on the fish quay. He played for North Shields AFC in centre forward position, receiving £15 per game. He had also played as centre forward on the Ralph Gardener school team. For North Shields AFC he trained twice a week, on a Monday and Wednesday evening, at their home ground of Appleby Park. Matches were played on a Saturday, sometimes with a mid-week evening game. On a couple of occasions he needed to leave Walkers early to play mid-week. Away games were at towns such as Whitby, Bridlington, Tow Law, Ferryhill and Spennymoor i.e. teams in the Northern League. The latter three listed are towns in County Durham.

When working for Bowers, John Ellis and Walkers, working days ran from Monday to Saturday. At Walkers, Tony and two other filleters clubbed together to buy a small coble called *Olympic*. Their coble was berthed just inside of Lloyd's jetty and used as

WALKERS
Walkers Fish Merchants premises, Vita House, fish quay, 11 November 1987. Tony worked for Walkers during 1974 - 1979

a hobby boat. They had a few lobster pots just outside the piers, perhaps up to a mile out around the rocks, and would all three go out together in the boat before their Walkers day shift started. They went out during the potting season and sometimes their coble broke down. Another coble, *Julie Karen*, towed them back to harbour. *Julie Karen* was owned by Jimmy Flett and their two cobles often left the river together in the morning – so Jimmy was nearby if *Olympic* had engine trouble. The trio of lads had a store in the old Tyne Brand building. Here they would make lobster pots during spare hours after work. They owned *Olympic* for about two years, but this was not really a commercial venture.

Tony worked at Walkers for five years until 1979. During his time with John Ellis and Walkers he absorbed much information about the business of buying, selling and processing fish. In 1977 he married North Shields girl Connie, from a local family. He was still living in North Shields at this time, moving from a small flat in Spence Terrace to Craster Road. In 1979 he joined Mars of Hull / Walter Offord; the former was the parent company of the latter which was a local business. The two companies then combined. With Mars of Hull, Tony's boss was Joe Stephenson, who later opened Kristian's fish and chip shop on the quay (where Oceans fish and chip restaurant is now located on Union Quay). For Mars he worked alongside the Caley's building, where Wright and Eddies is now located. Here he continued as a fish filleter and driver – making local deliveries to Ashington, Newbiggin, Bedlington, etc. They dealt in a range of fish including cod, haddock and coley. Tony worked there for two to three years, leaving in 1982 to set up his own business.

BOX OF HADDOCK
On North Shields fish quay market, a wooden Caley Fisheries fish box full of North Sea haddock, 9 September 1985

With an old school friend, called Vic Armstrong, Tony began a fish quay business. Firstly they sub-letted part of a unit from a chap called Hank and Peter Hope. This was where Taylor's shop now stands inside Clifford's Fort, but was then an old smokehouse. At first the pair had no business name. Vic was a plater by trade who had served his time with the Tyne Swan Hunter shipyard. The business pair bought odd boxes of fish off the market for Tony to fillet. They would then search the yellow pages phone directory to find any fish and chip shops who may take it. "We'd take a chance," Tony said. "First one we got was in Bedlington," he reported. As the duo continued they decided on a name for their business … AA Fisheries, with the two 'A's representing each of their surnames. So they attended the morning fish market, bought some fish and cut it to pre-pack into pound packs by weight. They went home for their tea, and in the evening travelled to Blyth, Ashington and Newbiggin, to pubs, clubs, hospitals – selling their fish, to return home by nine or ten o'clock. "It was long days," Tony remembered. They mainly dealt in cod and haddock, also selling smoked and baked herring. A wrapping machine was used to help them seal their goods. The smoked fish they sold came from Horn's smokehouse inside Clifford's Fort. After they had been trading for about a year there was a fire in their premises, and the smokehouse burnt down. "That was us wrecked!" Tony said. However they bounced back – moving in with a merchant at Vita House, directly below the clock. Here they worked, for a few months, inside part of the merchant's store, making use of a small space beside a large freezer. AA Fisheries was then offered a unit of their own on the road opposite, by a company called Dennis Bell. Dennis had four units, but two were unused, and AA Fisheries took both vacant units over following the offer. From here Tony and Vic sold a lot of pre-packs to some lads who sold them on. They became very busy and had three filleters working for them, with Tony and Vic occasionally filleting too. They had their own poppa, stored in their units. Tony bought fish from the market, loaded it onto their poppa and transported it to their store. The fish was then cut and packed for fish and chip shops and other outlets. "We had some decent orders," Tony recalled. AA Fisheries then bought a wet fish shop at an indoor market at Gateshead and a woman sold their fish on these premises.

By 1987 Tony had two sons, Anthony and Justin, and AA Fisheries had been in existence for five years. At this point the business pair split and went their own ways. Vic kept AA Fisheries while Tony started Seaview Fisheries inside Clifford's Fort at some new units. AA Fisheries continued successfully for many years, with Vic Armstrong in command, closing around 2001. This business had latterly moved to the fish quay Crescent of units (all now demolished), and employed several staff. Tony's new business started with a clear order book, but he gradually built a customer base. His brother John helped fillet for a while and the business progressed and started to supply a company called SeaFeast with small fillets of cod, whiting, lemon sole, etc. In early 1988 he bought the first part of his current premises on Union Quay as a wet fish shop. He purchased a single unit at first, from John Ward. This later extended into a four unit block – as Tony bought the neighbouring three units to knock through and make into larger premises. The three adjoining units were purchased from Neville

ON THE MARKET
Tony examines the fish for sale on the fish quay market on the morning of 22 September 1987. To the right of Tony stands fish merchant Alex Hastie M.B.E.

Hewison (owner of Hewison Seafoods). Tony had noted a decline in the wholesale fish trade by 1989, so decided to gear his business towards retail trade.

In 1989 Tony owned two Seaview Fisheries premises: one inside Clifford's Fort, which started trading in September 1987, and the other on Union Quay. He decided to add salmon processing to his premises inside the fort and began to employ six to seven staff for this part of his business. He travelled to Inverness and learnt about salmon processing. Then his Clifford's Fort business started to receive farmed fish from Wester Ross Seafoods, Inverness. Next door to his fort premises was a unit owned

UNION QUAY
The photograph shows some of the businesses on the main street, 11 January 1987. Eventually Tony took over all the John Reed premises, shown on the right of the photograph. He first started in these premises by taking over the wet fish shop (early 1988) at the left of the John Reed sign

FISH QUAY FESTIVAL
On left of photograph is Mark Higgins who slightly obscures Tony Asiamah. They are serving barbecued kippers outside Seaview Fisheries, Union Quay, 29 May 1988. Behind the flags in the upper left is Vita House, while the tall centre building is the top of the Old Low Light

SEAVIEW FISHERIES
Tony's business on Union Quay, North Shields fish quay, 16 November 2013. In front of the main window are two small tables and a folded chair – where the author (Daniel Turner) occasionally sells cards, fund-raising for Tynemouth RNLI lifeboat station

by Alan Longstaff, but Alan ceased trading and the unit became vacant. Tony took it over, knocking the two units into one. At these units work progressed to fillet and pack fish purchased off the fish quay market as well as processing the salmon from Scotland. At this time Tony's son Anthony joined the business, after serving time as a professional footballer with Newcastle United Football Club. He was aged 19 years. Tony's other son, Justin, played with Ipswich Town Football Club during 1997 - 2000. The boys' parents had encouraged their sons, and they both played with Wallsend Boys Club in their early years. Tony and his wife travelled widely, taking their sons to play in matches – all of the time watched by football scouts. While playing for Ipswich, Justin's ankles became damaged and brought about the end of his playing career. He now works in the North Sea offshore oil industry.

ANTHONY SIGNS FOR NUFC
Anthony Asiamah signs up with Newcastle United Football Club, 1994. Behind stand (from left): Pepe Goicoechea (Tony's father-in-law), Tony Asiamah (proud father!), Justin Asiamah (Tony's other son) and Chris McMenemy (First Team coach, NUFC, 1993 - 2000). Photograph courtesy of Tony Asiamah and with the permission of Newcastle United Football Club

When Anthony joined his father's business he was shown how to fillet and process salmon. "He's probably the best salmon processor on the fish quay now," Tony declared to the author. This salmon business was contract work for Wester Ross

Seafoods, and Seaview Fisheries filleted the fish to return to Inverness. Some of the filleted salmon was sent elsewhere, at the request of Wester Ross Seafoods, for example to Birmingham. His business continued to process cod, haddock, and other fish too. Supply to local fish and chip shops, many owned by Gills, kept the business very busy. Eventually the salmon order and processing dwindled. Therefore, in 2002, Tony decided to close his two Clifford's Fort units and bring his staff together at his other premises on Union Quay.

ANTHONY AND RAY'S BREAM
Anthony Asiamah prepares to fillet a Ray's Bream, Seaview Fisheries, 27 October 2010. The fish was found freshly washed up dead on Whitley Bay beach by Linda K Charlton during a beached bird survey (Northeast England Beached Bird Surveys Group)

Tony witnessed the reduction in local fish landings. When he first started at the quay he recalled there were occasions with over 3,000 boxes of fish for sale on the market. Nowadays he may see three or four days in a year when there are no fish for sale. This also prompted the decision to close the wholesale side of his business in Clifford's Fort and concentrate on the retail aspects at his wet fish shop. Here the public can view his staff filleting and enjoy the extensive displays of fish.

Seaview Fisheries supplies currently originate from North Shields, Grimsby, Scrabster, Peterhead, Aberdeen, and Cornwall with further supplies from Norway and Russia. The former locations provide daily overnight deliveries, while the two latter locations

supply fish frozen, headless and gutted – mainly for the fish and chip trade. The latter supplies are thawed and filleted at Seaview Fisheries, and dispatched to many local chippies at places such as Sunderland, Durham and Newcastle. Such daily deliveries are sent from Seaview Fisheries, using their own transport and driver. At first this business also supplied to London and Birmingham, but now he cannot get sufficient supplies to send, due to the lower landings of fish. Local North Sea landings have diminished due to changes in quota allowances and the impact of over-fishing. Tony mentioned to the author about the influx of boats to North Shields in the winter prawn season – with so many vessels dragging fishing gear across the sea bed they are damaging the grounds. "It is only a matter of time before there is little left at all," he predicts.

Tony and his Seaview Fisheries staff have met many celebrities over the years while trading at the fish quay. For example, around 2010 *The Hairy Bikers* came to film. This is a popular BBC television cooking programme featuring two motorcycling men with long hair and beards … David Myers and Simon King. Tony accompanied them onto the morning market to buy some fish, returning to Tony's shop to cut it. The two characters then bought some other products from Seaview Fisheries, before cooking everything under the market sheds. Another example was when a television company contacted Tony when he was trading in Clifford's Fort. Mel B, one of the performers and singers from the Spice Girls (an all-girl pop group), got in touch to say they were making a short BBC-funded drama called *Fish* (2000; Director: Bruce Goodison) and asked if they could use the premises. At this time Seaview was processing salmon. So Mel B (also known as *Scary Spice*) came and dressed in all the garb of a fish processor, with wellies, leggings, etc., and was filmed handling the salmon. Salmon fillets are quite delicate and easily damaged. Tony laughed as he told the author, "She still owes us a few quid for breaking the salmon!" Famous footballers who have visited his store to purchase their fishy wares include: Jackie Charlton, David Ginola, Nobby Solano and Craig Bellamy. The latter three have played for Newcastle United at some point in their careers. Jackie Charlton (born at Ashington, Northumberland)

OPPOSITE:
PRAWNS ON SALE
Bright Norwegian prawns for sale at Tony's fish quay shop, 16 August 2014

LOCAL SALMON
Locally-caught wild salmon on sale in season, Seaview Fisheries, 16 August 2014

MACKEREL
On sale in Seaview Fisheries, full of oily goodness, 16 August 2014

SUNFISH SURPRISE!
North Shields fish quay, early morning market, 3 December 2012. Tony eyes up a sunfish for sale. He bought it for £24, but it turned out to be rotten and only suitable for disposal! From left: Phil Coltherd (Taylors Seafood), John Strasshine (JGS), Terry Reed (Caley Fisheries auctioneer), Jeremy Pritchard (Fish Quay Manager), Tony Asiamah and Ian Riches (J R Fisheries)

managed Newcastle United between 1984 and 1985, and played for England from 1965 - 1970. When Tony's son, Anthony, was with Newcastle United Football Club there were a couple of occasions when First Team player David Ginola asked him to mind his young child. Another well-known gentleman … British chef Keith Floyd, who featured in many television cookery shows, visited the fish quay many years ago to buy fish from the market. While visiting, he and Tony enjoyed a fishy conversation.

WILD SALMON
£18.00 KILO

KING PRAWNS
US SIZE
£24.00 KILO

BREAM
£8.50 KILO

WHOLE
RAINBOW TROUT
£5.50 KILO

SQUID TUBES
£7.50 KILO

FRESH SCALLOPS
£28.00 KILO

ATTRACTIVE DISPLAY
Part of the sales display in Seaview Fisheries,
16 August 2014

SMOKEHOUSE STAFF
The staff pause outside Tony's smokehouse.
From left: Tommy Cottingham, David Hamil
('Hammy') and Tony Asiamah (owner /
manager). 10 October 2014

Seaview Fisheries current staff comprise: Tony, his wife Connie, their son Anthony, nephew Darren, Connie's sister Ann, a newcomer to the fish shop Ellen Mundy, driver John Cox and top fish filleter Davy Smith. Davy taught Tony to fillet when they both worked for John Ellis in the 1970s. Another long-time member of staff was Stan

SEAVIEW FISHERIES STAFF
Outside the premises on Union Quay, 10 October 2014. From left: Connie Asiamah, Ann Goicoechea, Tony Asiamah, Anthony Asiamah, Davy Smith and Darren Asiamah

Fenwick, who retired in 2010 after working in the wet fish shop for 20 years. Stan, who is married to Connie's sister Chris, had worked for 25 years at Hoults the butchers, on Meadowell Estate, before starting at Seaview Fisheries when they commenced on Union Quay. Tony opened a nearby smokehouse in late 2013 – for the provision of supplies to his wet fish shop. Filleters Tommy Cottingham and 'Hammy' (David Hamil) work at the smokehouse. They currently smoke cod, haddock, herring and salmon. This farmed salmon comes from Scotland while the herrings are supplied from Grimsby and locally-sourced when in season.

Trevor F Fryer

Retired Tynemouth lifeboat volunteer, awarded RNLI Bronze Medal in 1974

In 1956 Frederick Harry Fryer and his wife Louise with their children Trevor and Shirley moved to Tyneside. Frederick came to join the coastguard service based in the grounds of the castle at Tynemouth, after spending 28 years in the navy where he had been a gunnery instructor. He served throughout the Second World War and had been on the battleship *HMS Barham* when she was torpedoed (25 November 1941) in the Mediterranean. As well as serving in the Mediterranean fleet during the war Frederick also served with the arctic fleet and in the Middle East. So in 1956 the family moved to Battery Point beside the Haven, Tynemouth, where five coastguards lived at that time. Trevor's father retired at the age of 65 and died seven years later, aged 72, of lung cancer. He and his crew-mates used to sleep in hammocks below the large eighteen or twenty-four inch guns on various battleships and when the guns above were fired the asbestos lagging under the guns "used to come down like snow," said Trevor, which obviously the men breathed and contributed to Frederick's ill health.

Frederick H Fryer became involved with the Golden Sands Club along with Percy A Appleby, a local fishmonger situated at the entrance to the fish quay Gut, and other business people ... "My dad got in cahoots with local businesses" was how Trevor put it. The Golden Sands Club "must have been the largest raffle in the area at the time," and raised money for various good causes and Trevor recalls screwing up

PORTRAIT
At the Spanish Battery, Tynemouth with the Black Middens behind, at low tide, and the High and Low Lights beyond at North Shields fish quay, 19 Aug 2012

159

FREDERICK HARRY FRYER
Trevor's father on retirement.
Photograph courtesy of Trevor Fryer

raffle tickets at home to put in a big drum to be drawn at The Plaza, Tynemouth, one of the main venues for their events. Trevor also recalled Tommy Sylph who was a sign-writer, in the 1950s and 1960s, based at the fish quay, also creating the signs for many local businesses. Trevor mentioned that Tommy had lived in Kirton Park Terrace opposite *The Gunner* public house in North Shields and ran a little Morris Eight van.

Often Trevor would see Ken Middlemiss, the Tynemouth lifeboat Honorary Secretary, walking at Battery Point and Collingwood's Monument. In the early 1960s Ken mentioned that they were to get an inshore boat at the Tynemouth station to augment the larger offshore vessel and therefore younger crew members would be needed. Meanwhile the Tynemouth lifeboat mechanic for the large boat at the fish quay, Frank Ide, moved into one of the old army houses at Battery Point. Frank only had a bicycle so Trevor, who then owned a van, would give Frank a lift to the lifeboat house at North Shields when called out on service. "Frank was born in Hastings and had a German wife and two sons," Trevor recounted as he showed me a lovely sailing boat in a bottle which Frank had made and was resting on a windowsill at the back of Trevor's home. Frank had sported a thick beard and would often exclaim "Bugger that!" in his rolling south country accent while Trevor recalled that at times Frank would get a meal of prawns from the fish quay caught up in his bushy beard and would need to pick them out.

So Trevor started helping with the Tynemouth inshore lifeboat in 1963. At that time he was working for R. Jordan's Ltd, a builder based at the back of Queen Alexandra Road, North Shields. Richard Jordan's business carried out much work for banks, hospitals and factories … for example the area around West Chirton Industrial Estate and the Formica factory on the nearby Coast Road. Jordan's were part of a factory group (possibly called 'Northern Industrial Estates') and they tackled work around North Shields, Blyth and Ashington. However Trevor's main work with them was with local banks, for example at 23 Front Street, Tynemouth – a bank (where Ian Sharp Antiques later traded for 25 years from 1988) located on the north side of the street; he worked on the premises for a while before it was opened for business. The workmen had ensured the bank's wooden counter was highly polished and gleaming as a final touch for the opening day, only for one of the incoming cashiers carrying a large leather money bag with studs on the base to place it on the new counter and leave deep tram lines as it was dragged across the pristine woodwork. Ian Sharp (of Ian Sharp Antiques), recalled the premises was a bank from 1959 - 1986, housing the Midland Bank when Ian purchased the property in January 1988.

From Jordan's Trevor progressed to the County Borough of Tynemouth Engineers Department where he remained for 43 years until retirement in 2010. Trevor began with the Engineers Department as a joiner and ended as a maintenance technician. As part of this work Trevor repaired fish quay store doors "scores of times" when break-ins took place overnight on a regular basis. The work had to be completed during the next working day so that the business could lock their premises securely at close of play that evening. The thieves would steal fish after breaking down the outer doors fairly quietly by using various vehicles. The fish quay newspaper shop and other offices there were also broken into frequently, often with the thieves breaking through the ceiling above thereby avoiding the warning wires protecting doors and

TYNESIDER
Lifeboat *Tynesider* served with Tynemouth lifeboat station during 1947 - 1979. Photograph courtesy of Tynemouth lifeboat station archives

windows. Trevor worked from the Hudson Street Council Depot in North Shields and would make repairs following such activities. He also cleared up after school break-ins, for example at Ralph Gardner's School (Chirton) the kitchen windows would be used as a point of entry by the miscreants and Trevor and his gang would need to clean away the scattered glass from inside the kitchen, replace the windows and tidy up associated damage so school meals could be made.

Trevor's initial experience with the Tynemouth lifeboats was with the early inshore boat and *Tynesider* – a 47 feet Watson class non-self-righting vessel. Trevor recalled that initially *Tynesider* had no wheelhouse, but one was added later under the first such modification made in the country. This modification was carried out at Littlehampton and Trevor recounted "there was no radar aboard in those days," and that *Tynesider* had been bought with local funds after the old lifeboat house at Fish Quay Sands was bombed in April 1941. He and the other lifeboat crew built a brick lifeboat house for the inshore boat above Fish Quay Sands, beside the crew's storage house. This first inshore lifeboat house opened facing the river, with a small slipway in front. However a severe storm washed away this building. They later rebuilt in the same spot, this time with a thick gable end facing seawards, to protect the building in a heavy sea, and an opening for the entry and exit of the boat, but facing upriver instead of directly river-facing. This second inshore lifeboat house remained sound until demolition many years later following movement of the inshore boat to its current location at the eastern end of the fish quay market. A 52 feet Barnett class lifeboat called *Princess Alexandra* was on service at North Shields for two years, replacing *Tynesider*, before the new Arun class lifeboat *George and Olive Turner* (52-13) came into service at North Shields in 1980.

Trevor has a photograph of a Dutch dredger *Beverwijk III* that came aground in November 1965 at the base of the northern side of Tynemouth pier. The photograph shows the crew from the dredger walking along the arm of the ship's massive crane to step off safely onto the pier. Trevor showed the author another photograph of some lifeboat crew aboard *Tynesider* – in ceremonial red woollen hats and white ganseys – on their way to Blyth Harbour for the lifeboat open day. They would also visit Cullercoats on such harbour days, which the current lifeboat continues to do. In this photo Ken Middlemiss is present polishing some brasses. Trevor explained another photograph, taken on *Tynesider,* showing "coxswain Bobby Brunton, who lived in Cullercoats and Bob (Robert) Mackenzie who was second coxswain in those days."

RNLI BRONZE MEDAL FOR GALLANTRY
Awarded to Trevor Fryer for the Tynemouth lifeboat service on 10 March 1974 following the grounding of oil rig support ship *Oregis* and tug *Northsider* in terrible conditions

RNLI BRONZE MEDAL
Obverse side

MEDAL PRESENTATION
Trevor Fryer receiving his bronze medal for gallantry from HRH The Duke of Kent at the Royal Festival Hall in London. The presentation was on 8 May 1975. Photograph courtesy of RNLI

For a rescue with the inshore lifeboat (D 172) on Sunday 10 March 1974, helmsman Trevor was awarded the Bronze Medal of the RNLI for taking off the crew from tug *Northsider* that ran aground on the Black Middens during terrible conditions following the engine breakdown of oil rig exploration ship *Oregis* when leaving the river in the afternoon. The tug got into difficulties in the strong easterly wind (force 6-7), rough sea and high swell on going to assist the *Oregis* (which was crewed by 40 persons). Three tugs went to help the *Oregis*, but *Northsider* was driven by the heavy sea onto the rocks. Experienced lifeboat man Fred Arkley crewed the inshore boat with Trevor and was also awarded the RNLI bronze medal for his part in the rescue. Fred and Trevor had noticed the *Oregis* in difficulty in the river mouth at 15.30 GMT and quickly launched the inshore boat, skipping the normal protocol of requesting permission to launch. Within minutes the *Oregis* and *Northsider* were grounded on the Black Middens and the two lifeboat men took a boy, the son of one of the tug's crew, off the tug returning an hour later on receiving a request to rescue the remaining crew of three. It took a few attempts to take off the tug crew due to the harsh weather tossing the tug around as she lay grounded on rocks close below the surface – and in danger of breaking up. The rescued boy was taken to hospital, but sent home later in the day. The Deputy Director of the RNLI wrote thus to Trevor … 'The Committee were impressed by the courage and determination displayed by you in carrying out this rescue and it was decided to award you the bronze medal of the Institution. You will also receive a vellum recording the award. … … I should like to take this opportunity to send you my personal congratulations on your well-deserved award and to express my admiration of this fine service.' Trevor and Fred were presented with their medals by HRH The Duke of Kent (RNLI president) at the Royal Festival Hall, London on 8 May 1975 and were invited to the Houses of Parliament. Trevor was accompanied by his mother and sister. "This was great!" remarked Trevor as he was able to enjoy a bird's eye view of the parliamentary proceedings below from the Visitors Gallery. Following the rescue Trevor received letters of congratulations from Tynemouth MP Neville Trotter and Mr T A Heatley, Chief Engineer of North Tyneside Council in whose department Trevor worked. Lifeboat man Fred Arkley, who was a Tyne foy-boatman, had helped cast off the *Oregis* from her river berth shortly before she broke down while leaving the river. Fred died from cancer in later years. The *Oregis* was re-floated on the afternoon of Monday 8 April 1974 on the eighth such attempt since she went aground. On seven of these re-floating attempts the RNLI records show Tynemouth inshore lifeboat (D 172) was launched and stood by. Trevor was helmsman on six of these seven attempts, including the successful one. When she was re-floated there was a NE force 2-3 wind (improving the predicted tide) and smooth sea, but 'thick fog came down'. The service log

NEVILLE TROTTER, B.Com., F.C.A., M.P., J.P.

HOUSE OF COMMONS
LONDON SWIA OAA

May, 1974

T. Fryer, Esq.,
Coastguard Cottages,
TYNEMOUTH.

Dear Mr. Fryer,

I was interested to read you had recently been awarded a Bronze Medal for the part you played in the rescue operation when a tug went aground on the Black Middens.

I understand 3 men and a boy were rescued from the tug and the medals were awarded to yourself and Mr. Arkley for your prompt action in saving these people.

This medal is truly well deserved and I send you my congratulations and best wishes for the future.

Yours sincerely,

Neill Trotter

LETTER FROM MP
Letter of congratulations from Tynemouth MP Neville Trotter, May 1974

records that 'river tugs assisted the vessel up channel towards safe berth.' It seems the compass was very useful on the ILB during the fog! During his time as a volunteer with the RNLI Trevor attended two garden parties at Buckingham Palace, one of which was on 16 July 1974 … on that occasion held to mark the 150th Anniversary of the RNLI. The Lifeboat (Journal of the RNLI) of autumn 1974 (No 449, pages 215-216) recorded the rescue. The presentation of the medals is recorded in The Lifeboat

OREGIS
Oil rig support ship *Oregis* lies grounded off the Spanish Battery, in the Tyne river mouth, March 1974

NORTHSIDER
Tug *Northsider* founders on the Black Middens at high tide, March 1974

edition of Summer 1975 (No 452, pages 9-15) under the Annual General Meeting section with a sub-title of '1974 – A year of triumph'.

One of the events recalled by Trevor from his time with the lifeboat involved the *Ganton*, a merchant cargo ship that ran aground at St Mary's Island, on 14 December 1979, after the captain thought he was off Souter. Trevor and Jimmy Griffiths crewed the inshore lifeboat (ILB) and took off three of the crew of six – one came down the ladder with a black eye and carrying a blaring ghetto blaster perched on his shoulder. Trevor asked how he got the black eye. "The skipper hit me!" came the retort. Apparently the crew had been drunk that night! The wind was a northerly force 5 and the red inshore lifeboat (D 172) was launched at 06:20 as a boarding boat for the all-weather lifeboat (ALB) berthed at South Shields. ILB helmsman Trevor accompanied the ALB, keeping her in sight at all times, before arrival at the casualty at 07:00. The three crew members, who were taken off by the ILB, were transferred to the ALB and landed later, but the rest of the crew from the *Ganton* remained aboard her for the time being as further crew transfer was becoming too hazardous. The tide

*That the Thanks of the
Royal National Life-boat Institution
be accorded to
Trevor Fryer
Helmsman of the Tynemouth D class inflatable life-boat
in recognition of the determination and seamanship
displayed by him when the life-boat rescued nine people
from the motor boat 'Blue Fin'
which had broken down off Trow Point
and was subsequently wrecked on the rocks
in a strong northerly wind and a rough breaking sea
on the 11th April, 1982*

BLUE FIN VELLUM
Thanks on vellum accorded to Trevor Fryer for the rescue of nine people from the *Blue Fin* – which was later wrecked on the rocks off South Shields

was rising and the service records state 'The *Ganton* was close inshore with a NE sea running in and breaking at times along the ship's side.' The ILB was returned to the lifeboat station at 11:45 a.m. and the *Ganton* was re-floated on 18 December.

For an inshore service as helmsman of the D class lifeboat on 11 April 1982 Trevor was accorded the Thanks of the Institution inscribed on vellum, also receiving a badge as a memento of the occasion. During this service nine people were rescued from the motor boat *Blue Fin* which was drifting onto Trow Rocks, South Shields, after engine failure. In addition Trevor received a letter from the chief executive and county clerk of Tyne and Wear County Council concerning this rescue. The letter states 'You may be aware the County Council has a scheme to make awards to any person who performs a commendable act of bravery or gallantry. I am pleased to inform you that the County Council have awarded you a Gold Medal and a cheque for £50 in recognition of your act of bravery at the above incident.' The medal and cheque were presented at the County Council meeting of Wednesday 23 February 1983 at 2 p.m. at the town hall and civic centre, Sunderland. Trevor had been nominated for the award, without his knowledge, by two people he knew: Robert Brunton (ex-coxswain of Tynemouth lifeboat) and David Tuff (chief technician / engineer, British Rail signals). The RNLI recorded their thanks on vellum for this service incorporating the words '... accorded to Trevor Fryer Helmsman of the Tynemouth D class inflatable life-boat in recognition of the determination and seamanship displayed by him when the life-boat rescued nine people from the motor boat *Blue Fin* which had broken down off Trow Point and was subsequently wrecked on the rocks in a strong northerly wind and a rough breaking sea on 11th April, 1982.' The inshore lifeboat was launched at 15:22, on the authorisation of the honorary secretary, in cold conditions with a force 6 northerly wind

GOLD MEDAL FOR BRAVERY
Awarded to Trevor Fryer by Tyne and Wear County Council in recognition of his pivotal role in the *Blue Fin* rescue

and heavy sea ... reaching the casualty at 15:30. Lifeboat man Stuart Brown was the second crew member of the inshore lifeboat with Trevor. *Blue Fin* had anchored after drifting close to the shore and the service records state 'The casualty swung about wildly in the seas.' 'Helmsman ... decided it was unwise to wait for the Arun arriving, anchor rope was very thin and under great strain. At any time the casualty could part and drive ashore in minutes, beyond rescue (the seas were crashing straight up the

30 - 40 feet cliffs). Carefully sizing up the seas, helmsman made a run and got close alongside, asked all the crew (5 visible) to jump immediately, then 4 more appeared from cabin, all were taken aboard and ILB got clear as quickly as possible.' By now the heavy load on the lifeboat meant her speed was reduced to about two knots and Trevor 'had great difficulty in coaxing her up and over some very steep seas,' and was taking aboard and bailing a lot of water. The inshore lifeboat continued to the lifeboat station, arriving at 15:55, 'where men were safely landed, all full of praise and very grateful for their rescue from a fate which was obvious to them all.' The large all-weather Arun lifeboat checked on the *Blue Fin* which soon broke up under the cliffs. In the service records, lifeboat station honorary secretary, Ken Middlemiss, recorded 'Had he [Trevor] not taken the actions when he did there is every chance casualty would have been destroyed and all in her drowned before Arun could assist.'

LA MORLAYE
Fishing vessel *La Morlaye* (LH 207) lies in the Gut at the fish quay behind *Lady Zena*, 5 October 1985. She was the subject of a RNLI silver medal rescue in the early hours of 15 April 1986 off Whitley Bay beach – she soon broke up

Trevor received a letter of appreciation for his fine efforts, from the RNLI Chief of Operations, for a rescue in the D class inflatable lifeboat on 12 January 1986. Three children were cut off by the tide in a small bay south of Marsden Rock and Trevor was helmsman for the service. The letter expands … 'It is noted that the lifeboat launched and proceeded in very rough seas to the area where the three boys were trapped, where the beach was steep and stony with many off-lying rocks partially awash, thus making the approach particularly hazardous. Crew members J. Griffiths and S. Brown entered the water, steadied the lifeboat and carried the boys out to it to be rescued and brought safely to shore.'

Trevor was a crew man on Tynemouth lifeboat *George and Olive Turner* during the rescue of the crew of three from disabled fishing vessel *La Morlaye* (LH 207, 59 feet length) in the early hours of 15 April 1986 off Whitley Bay. The fishing vessel's propellers were fouled in her gear and she was being driven aground less than 400 yards from the shore in twenty feet high rollers and surf, the wind was ESE gale force 8. The fishing vessel had been towed 27 miles from the fishing grounds, but the tow had parted to be re-connected by another fishing vessel, but was now closing on the shore and the coastguard was called for assistance. The lifeboat left her berth at 01:15 (after the crew were paged at 01:03), following authorisation to launch by the Honorary Secretary Ken Middlemiss, and reached the casualty at 01:28. During the lifeboat rescue three attempts to tow *La Morlaye* resulted in snapped tow lines

LIFEBOAT DEMONSTRATION
The RAF Sea King rescue helicopter lowers a crew member to *RNLB George and Olive Turner* (52-13). Photograph taken on 28 May 1989 during the Fish Quay Festival

due to the violent motion of the boats and sea, one snapped line 'whipped back and hit lifeboatman David Lisle bruising his leg.' During the second attempt to tow 'Second Coxswain Martin Kenny, who was on the stern about to throw the rope, was thrown across the guard rails, but was pulled to safety by the crew.' Weighing up the dangers, coxswain John Hogg managed to get the lifeboat alongside the fishing vessel and 'Although the boats were rising and falling 20 feet, two men jumped onto the lifeboat head first and the third was hauled aboard by the lifeboatmen.' On the return passage 'the survivors were kept warm in the cabin, covered with blankets and given a lot of brandy.' The lifeboat left the fishing vessel at 02:10 and had returned to station by 02.27 a.m., was then refuelled and made ready for service. *La Morlaye* was 'driven up [the] beach on a rising tide, in two pieces by high water and broke up totally next tide', records the service log book. Honorary Secretary Ken Middlemiss included his own further remarks in the return of service RNLI log book 'Having regard to the severe conditions which prevailed throughout, the very close proximity of the rocks, and the fact that no other assistance was available, I am sure the 3 would have been swept into the surf within a few moments. Recommend you please carefully consider an award for this very fine service. KM.' For this service coxswain John A Hogg was presented with the silver bravery medal of the RNLI and

EᴵᴵR

The Lord Chamberlain is commanded by Her Majesty to invite

Mr. Trevor Fryer.

to an Afternoon Party in the Garden of Buckingham Palace to mark the 150th Anniversary of the Royal National Life-Boat Institution on Tuesday, the 16th July 1974, from 4 to 6 p.m.

Lounge Suit

GARDEN PARTY INVITATION
To Buckingham Palace, 16 July 1974

LIFEBOAT RETIREES
Enjoying a natter at Tynemouth lifeboat station. From left: Captain Leonard Park (lifeboat helper), Stuart Brown (crew) and Trevor Fryer (crew). Photograph taken on 11 May 2008

framed medal service certificates were presented to the rest of the crew i.e. second coxswain Martin Kenny, mechanic Joseph Watson, and crew members Trevor Fryer, John Norris, James Griffiths and David Lisle.

On 27 May 1986 Trevor crewed, with helmsman Stuart Brown, the inshore lifeboat when fishing coble *James Denyer* drifted onto the Black Middens in a westerly gale after suffering engine failure. Both Stuart and Trevor received letters with grateful thanks from the RNLI Chief of Operations. Refer to Stuart Brown's section in this book for further details.

On one 1987 trip Trevor picked up a lifeboat from Poole, Dorset, and took her to La Coruña in Spain for the XVth International Lifeboat Conference. For this he received a letter of thanks from the Director of the RNLI, Rear Admiral W J Graham CB MNI

– in which the Rear Admiral states '... I should like to thank you very much for all you did to ensure the RNLI was so well represented. The lifeboat and her crew were a credit to the RNLI in La Coruña and marvellous ambassadors for your country and the lifeboat service.'

ROYAL NATIONAL LIFEBOAT INSTITUTION

FOR THE PRESERVATION OF LIFE FROM SHIPWRECK

ESTABLISHED IN 1824

CERTIFICATE OF SERVICE

THIS IS TO CERTIFY

THAT

T. F. Fryer

*served as Second Coxswain
and a crew member
of the Tynemouth Lifeboats
for a total of 36½ years, during which period
the Lifeboats rescued 288 lives from shipwreck.
The Committee of Management
are glad to place on record this testimony
to his personal participation in
the Lifeboat Service.*

Bronze Medal 1974

David Acland
Chairman

November 1999

Director

RNLI CERTIFICATE OF SERVICE
This records a marvellous 36 and a half years of service as a volunteer with the Tynemouth lifeboats

Trevor received recognition for 25 years of service with Tynemouth Inshore Lifeboat in a letter dated 18 July 1990 from Lieut. Commander B Miles RD MNI RNR, Director of the RNLI, when retiring from service with the inshore lifeboat. This letter concluded 'I am delighted to learn that you are to remain as Second Coxswain of the Arun and I thank you for your continuing support of the Institution's work.' Trevor had however served a little longer than 25 years with the inshore lifeboat by then, having commenced such duties in 1963.

Trevor received another letter of thanks from the Director of the RNLI (Lieut. Commander Brian Miles) for a rescue on 3 March 1990 when a crew of seven aboard the *George and Olive Turner* rescued an exhausted board sailor within the Tyne harbour entrance – the man had been reported missing. The service was from 17:14 – 17:55 GMT in a 'North Westerly Force seven wind' with the board sailor sighted by lifeboat searchlight at 17:25 without his board and close to the South pier. The casualty was 'successfully pulled into the well of the lifeboat' on the second attempt, and he was 'close to unconsciousness.' The coxswain on this service was Martin A Kenny with Trevor acting as second coxswain, mechanic Kevin J Mole, assistant mechanic Geoffrey Cowans, plus crew members James Edward H Griffiths, David Lisle and Andrew Keady. The letter concludes 'This service was conducted in a very professional manner, and on behalf of the Institution I send you my warm and appreciative thanks for a

At a meeting of the Committee of Management of the

ROYAL NATIONAL
LIFE-BOAT INSTITUTION
FOR THE PRESERVATION OF LIFE FROM SHIPWRECK
held at their offices, London, on the 8th day of May, 1974,
the following minute
was ordered to be recorded on the books of the Institution

That the Bronze Medal of the
Royal National Life-boat Institution
be awarded to
Trevor Fryer

A member of the crew of the Tynemouth inshore life-boat
in recognition of the courage, seamanship and
determination displayed by him when the inshore
life-boat under his command rescued a boy and
the crew of three from the tug "Northsider"
which had gone ashore on the rocks near
Freestone Point at the entrance to the River
Tyne in a strong easterly wind and a rough
sea with a heavy swell on the afternoon of
the 10th March, 1974.

F.R.H.Swann
Chairman

President

Director and Secretary

RNLI BRONZE MEDAL VELLUM
Recording Trevor's courage during the Tynemouth lifeboat service on 10 March 1974

BRONZE MEDAL PRESENTATION
Frederick Arkley receiving his Bronze medal for gallantry from HRH The Duke of Kent at the Royal Festival Hall in London. The presentation was on 8 May 1975 to mark the lifeboat service in the Tyne river mouth on 10 March 1974. Photograph courtesy of RNLI

FAMILY PHOTO
Trevor with his mother (Louise Elsie), following the presentation of his and Fred's RNLI Bronze medals. Photograph courtesy of Trevor Fryer

fine team effort, carried out in darkness and difficult conditions in the confines of the harbour entrance.'

On a further rescue, Trevor recounted that the lifeboat "followed a string of green beer bottles floating in the sea for 26 miles to rescue a Polish fishing vessel offshore." At the time several Polish boats fished in the area and the crew drank this beer, which was not from Britain, and would throw the bottles overboard. Once, when just off the Tyne piers, Trevor witnessed the *George and Olive Turner* covered in birds, "You

could not walk on deck for the birds," he said, "I think Michael Nugent was on board that day." Another rescue involving the Arun class lifeboat was when she arrived just in time to rescue the crew from their sinking fishing boat just outside the piers, again during dense fog in daylight. The skipper was last to leave his boat and he stepped onto the lifeboat just as his vessel sank. In November 1999 Trevor retired as a volunteer from the Tynemouth lifeboat crew after 36 and a half years of dedicated service during which the Tynemouth lifeboats rescued 288 lives. During this time Trevor had served as crew member, helmsman of the inshore lifeboat and second coxswain of the all-weather lifeboat.

TREVOR AND THE BLACK MIDDENS
Over-looking the Tyne river mouth and notorious Black Middens – the scene of many a shipwreck, 19 August 2012

References

British Ornithologists Union

Debretts, Biographies, www.debretts.com

Football information, (information about Brian Powton – for Kevin Mole's account):
    a. http://www.nufc.com
    b. http://www.neilbrown.newcastlefans.com

Hedges, Nick: photographer, www.workinglife.org.uk

Loud, Peter: photographer, http://www.peterloud.co.uk/photos/photos.html

Marine Accident Investigation Branch (MAIB), Report No 15/2005, August 2005

Maritime and Coastguard Agency:
    MSN 1770 (F) Merchant Shipping Notice 1770 (F):
        The Fishing Vessels Code of Safe Working Practice for the Construction and
        Use of 15-24 metre Fishing Vessels (Effective from 23 November 2002);
    SI 2002   Fishing Vessels (Safety of 15–24 Metre Vessels) Regulations SI 2002;

Ministry of Agriculture, Fisheries and Food:
    Macer, C.T. & Burd, A.C. March 1970. Fishing for sandeels, Leaflet No 21,
    http://www.cefas.defra.gov.uk/publications/lableaflets/lableaflet21.pdf

North Shields Library, Local Studies resource centre

Pears, Brian: 1994-2008. Rowlands Gill and the North-East 1939 – 1945, Chapter 8 Attacks on the North-East. http://www.bpears.org.uk/Misc/War_NE/w_section_08.html

Ripley, R & Pears, B, 1994-2011. North-East Diary 1939 – 1945, Incidents 28th April 1941 to 7th/8th May 1941. http://www.ne-diary.bpears.org.uk/Inc/ISeq_18.html

RNLI Archive, RNLI Heritage Trust, Poole, Dorset.

RNLI Film and Image unit

Seahouses RNLI Lifeboat Operations Manager, Ian Clayton - station archive information

Side Publications, Newcastle upon Tyne. (1988). North Shields Fish Quay and Fishing Industry, Exhibition pack.

Tyne and Wear Archives, Discovery Museum, Blandford Square, Newcastle upon Tyne

Tynemouth RNLI Lifeboat Station, archives

Tynemouth Life-boat 90th Anniversary 1862 – 1952, Souvenir brochure. Cail & Sons Ltd, Quayside, Newcastle upon Tyne

Wikipedia, Internet:
      Sinking of the *Christine Nielsen*:
            http://www.maib.gov.uk/cms_resources.cfm?file=/christine-nielsen-text.pdf
      Control Commission for Germany – British Element:
            http://en.wikipedia.org/wiki/Allied-occupied_Germany
      Uffa Fox, boat designer:
            http://en.wikipedia.org/wiki/Uffa_Fox

Wikipedia pages for:
      Footballers: Jackie Charlton, David Ginola, Nobby Solano and Craig Bellamy
      Others: The Hairy Bikers, Mel B (Spice Girls), various others

Wright, R. 2002. The People's History, Cullercoats (Not just a village, a unique place to live). Published by The People's History Ltd, Seaham, County Durham.

Miscellaneous internet sites utilised

http://www.bpears.org.uk

http://www.ne-diary.bpears.org.uk

http://www.divemagazine.co.uk

http://uboat.net

http://www.theshipslist.com/ships/lines/bergen.htm

http://www.tynebuiltships.co.uk/R-Ships/reaveley1956.html

http://www.warsailors.com

http://en.wikipedia.org/wiki/TS_Leda

http://www.wrecksite.eu

There were many other internet searches carried out - while checking stories and background.

Acknowledgements

The author wishes to extend his grateful thanks to the following …

Brian Long – for kind permission to use two photographs (in Tony Asiamah's chapter)

Chiara Giulia Bertulli, Faxafloi Cetacean Research, University of Iceland – for kind permission to use her photograph of harbour porpoises (in Tommy Bailey's chapter)

Chris Morgan – for use of his photographs of (a) MS *Braemar,* and (b) the Fish Quay from *TS Leda* (in Rob Dearman's chapter)

Classic Boat Museum, East Cowes, Isle of Wight – for use of photograph and information about airborne lifeboats and Uffa Fox.

The Clive Ketley Collection – for photograph of the *Reaveley* (in Jackie Weatherstone's chapter)

Colin Alexander – for use of his dad's photograph of *T S Leda* (in Rob Dearman's chapter)

Fred. Olsen Cruise Lines – provision of advice and photograph of *Braemar I*

Gateshead Libraries – for photographs of Dunstan Staithes (in Rob Dearman's chapter)

George McVitie – for assistance with photographs, internet searches and website setup

Gordon Hyslop – for testing the author's White Wings Publishing website

Graham Relf – for help with website setup for White Wings Publishing

Ian Coombe, site manager (mnnostalgia.com), Merchant Navy Nostalgia – for kind permission to use photograph of mail ship *Apapa* (in Michael Smith's chapter)

Ian Fisher – provision of three bird photographs (in Eileen McConnell's chapter) and a minke whale photograph (in Tommy Bailey's chapter)

Ian Hancock and David Wright, Norfolk and Suffolk Aviation Museum (Flixton)

Ian Sharp   for information about his business premises when in Tynemouth Front Street

Linda K Charlton – for all her care and support as well as proof-reading

Michael Nugent – for allowing access to Tynemouth Lifeboat Station archive material, also for providing other local fishy and boat-related information

Michael Smith – for kind permission to allow use of images from some of his paintings

National Museums Liverpool, John Winrow – Assistant Curator

Newcastle United Football Club – for permission to use a photograph (in Tony Asiamah's chapter)

Nick Hedges – for kind permission to use two photographs (in Tony Asiamah's chapter)

Office of the Naval Secretary, Portsmouth

ncjMedia Ltd (Newcastle Chronicle and Journal) – for use of photograph of RNLI & RAF rescue at Cullercoats (in Stuart Brown's chapter)

Peter Loud – for use of two of his photographs (in Kevin Mole's chapter)

The Philip Simons Collection – for photograph of HM Customs Launch *Argus* (in Rob Dearman's chapter)

Raj Bhatia – for kind permission to use his portrait photograph of the author (back cover)

Ralph Robson – for bird taxidermy (Red Grouse Gallery, Rothbury)

Seahouses RNLI Lifeboat Station – for use of photograph of RNLB *Grace Darling*

The Shields Gazette (South Shields) – for use of the photograph of (RFA) *Tidereach*.

Swan Hunter (NE) Limited, John Mitchell

T.V.L.B. (Tynemouth Volunteer Life Brigade):
      a. Chris Lambert, historian (for information used in Eileen McConnell's chapter)
      b. Supply of photograph featuring Maurice McConnell

Tynemouth Photographic Society, Record Group, Stan Bewick & Howard Wilson

Tynemouth RNLI Lifeboat Station, for access to archives and use of some photographs

World Ship Society – Small Craft Group, Philip Simons – for his research and advice; also Alan Watt, Chatham Librarian at World Ship Society; and Tony Holtham

For their particular encouragement, advice and assistance: Linda K Charlton, Emma & Chris Hannen, Steve & Julie Holliday, Jeremy Pritchard, Ralph Thomas, Andrew & Simon Turner, … … and those to whom my book was mentioned (during its long gestation period) and who thought it was a good idea. Also to Heather Macpherson (Raspberry Creative Type) for all her advice and hard work – leading to such an attractive overall layout for the book; and to Donna Anderson and the staff of Elanders Ltd (printer) for their welcome help and attention.

With grateful thanks to all the 'folk' featured in this book – for allowing the author to record their stories for publication, allowing access to their records and for the freedom to record his subjects through photography. The subjects of this book also kindly allowed the author to include a selection of their own family and life photographs.

Please accept the author's apologies for any accidental omissions.

FISH QUAY SCENE
Fishing boats *Enterprise* and *Bethsaida* (HL 41; later renamed *Adaptable*) in the Gut, North Shields fish quay. The vessels belong to Dicky Leighton and rest below the Old High Light and Trinity Buildings, 13 May 2012

WING FEATHERS
Tips of the secondary feathers from the wing of a first year great black-backed gull – a regular bird of the Tyne estuary

HAKE ON ICE
A North Sea hake for sale at the fish quay, 3 December 2012

Fish Quay lifebelt